# Read 'em and Laugh

By
Max Shapiro

B&F Enterprises
Las Vegas, Nevada

Printed in the United States of America
First printing — July, 1995

Library of Congress Cataloging in Publication Data
Main entry under title:
Read 'em and Laugh

ISBN: 1-887816-00-3

Send inquiries to:
B & F Enterprises
1751 E. Reno Avenue, Suite 123
Las Vegas, Nevada 89119

Cover design and illustrations by Maryann Guberman

# DEDICATION

For my mother, Betty Shapiro,
who passed on to me her love of poker.

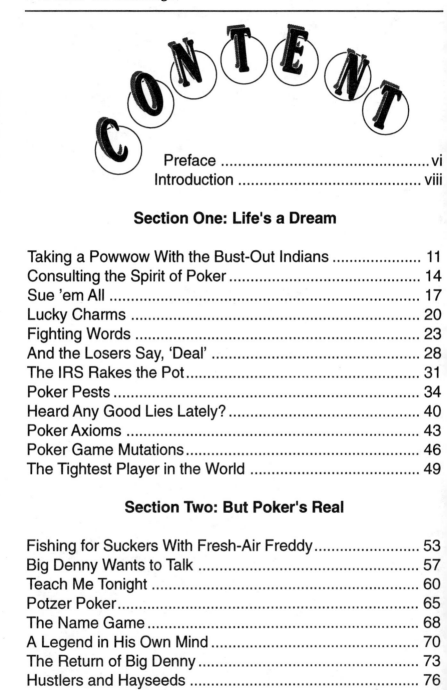

**Section Three: Where the Winners Tell Jokes**

**Section Four: And the Losers Say, 'Deal'**

# PREFACE

The humorous word is probably the toughest one to get on paper, not only because making people laugh is hard work, but also because when the writer is finished, there's no applause. There's no way to gauge whether or not the audience "got the joke."

Toss that together with the fact that gamblers, en masse — and in particular poker players — are not in the top ten in the category of belly laughers, and the job gets even tougher.

Few writers have been able to master gaming humor. Damon Runyon did the most notable job, though many readers often overlook that humor because of its melancholy nature. Runyon did it by peopling his stories with real characters off the street. As he chronicled life around him, real-world "degenerates" of the gambling world jumped into his fountain pen and splattered themselves all over his pages. The result was a splendid pandemonium mixed in with bittersweet drama.

Admittedly, when I first read Max Shapiro's work, I didn't think of Damon Runyon. I was behind a desk at a weekly Las Vegas tabloid called *Players Panorama.* Max was contributing articles that covered the poker scene in Southern California — the rules, the clubs, the games, the tournament action. It was, in short, the nuts and bolts of reporting. Sometimes, he would sneak in a little bit of instructional material. What I liked about his work was that it was clean, well-written, and on time. Every once in a while, he'd throw in a sentence or two that jumped out and tickled me, but humor was not the major focus of his words.

After that paper folded and I moved to a publication called *The Card Player*, Max's work surfaced there. And suddenly, I was chuckling again; sometimes I was laughing out loud. I soon discovered that lots of folks were laughing out loud when reading Max Shapiro's articles.

It wasn't until we were having coffee one evening after watching the *World Series of Poker* that I found out that Ralph the Rattler, Big Denny, and Fresh-Air Freddy, like Runyon's characters, were real people.

I badgered Max for years about putting together a collection of his best stories (and, of course, he thought *all* of his stories were his best). Finally, I told him I wanted to be involved in publishing it.

It still took two years to get it together, but *Read 'em and Laugh* is finally a reality. When you've finished reading it, you may not know much more about poker than when you started. You might not think about Damon Runyon, either, but that's OK because you'll surely know a whole lot about poker players — and about laughing.

Enjoy ...

Maryann Guberman

# INTRODUCTION

Most of the stories in *Read 'em and Laugh* have appeared in such publications as *Card Player, Players Panorama,* and *Whips and Bondage.* In some instances the articles have been rewritten and expanded so I could put back all the dirty parts that overzealous editors scrubbed out. This book also contains previously unpublished stories that nobody would print because they were considered too offensive, slanderous, or stupid.

It has been said that poker is America's favorite participant sport — though I suspect that Heidi Fleiss would argue otherwise. Some people play for recreation, some for money, and some just to get away from their spouses for a few hours. Whatever the reason, poker is an enduring part of American folklore, and the Friday night poker game is as much an American institution as apple pie and the O.J. Simpson trial.

I have played poker all my life — in casinos, in Army barracks, on boats, at the Los Angeles Press Club, in offices and garages, and at many, many home games where my opponents have included millionaire businessmen, bookies, noted actors, doctors, lawyers, police officers, and two brothers who later went to prison for hiring hit men to kill their parents.

Out of these encounters have come the inspiration for the stories in *Read 'em and Laugh.*

Are they true? Well, let's say even the most ludicrous ones contain a germ of truth. Those I sneezed on probably contain a lot of germs.

Sometimes events overtook what I wrote. In "Poker Game Mutations," I joked about a feminist deck of cards. Two years later some women began marketing just such a deck. In the "Bust-Out Indian" story I wove a fanciful tale of searching for an obscure Indian tribe to hustle into building a casino. Later I read a newspaper story about some hustler who did exactly the same thing.

Yet another time I offered some inconceivably outrageous "dirty tricks" ideas, only to get a threatening letter from an old reprobate named Dirty Wally who accused me of stealing all his moves.

Life does indeed imitate art, and sometimes it imitates poker, but don't try to imitate the stories in *Read 'em and Laugh* because they're copyrighted.

I hope you have as much fun reading 'em as I did writing 'em.

*Max Shapiro*

# SECTION ONE

# Life's a Dream ...

I have measured out my life with coffee spoons.
*T.S. Eliot*

I have measured out *mine* with antes and busted flushes.
*Max Shapiro*

# TAKING A POWWOW WITH THE BUST-OUT INDIANS

**M**any Indian tribes have amassed fortunes ever since Congress passed the *Indian Gaming Regulatory Act* that let them open casinos on their reservations. And that gave me one of my best ideas in years. If I could find a remote Indian tribe somewhere that hadn't yet heard about this bonanza, maybe I could negotiate a deal with them to open a casino and get rich beyond my wildest dreams.

To be honest, I didn't know much about Native Americans. I couldn't tell a Navajo from a Las Vegas ho.

But I did some research at the library, poring through the *Federal Register of Indian Tribes,* and sure enough, I came across an account of a lost tribe called the Bust-Out Indians. The Bust-Outs were degenerate gamblers who lost their reservation in 1880 to a bunch of card sharks in a crooked faro game and were last spotted somewhere up around Death Valley, still looking for a new stake.

So I drove to the desert and wandered around like Moses, hot on the spoor of the Bust-Outs. Finally, I crested a ridge one day and gazed down at a small band of natives engaged in what appeared to be their tribal rituals: They were pitching pennies, dealing cards, and betting on which yucca tree a buzzard would land on.

My quest was over!

I scrambled down the hill and approached one of the tribesmen who was clad in stone-washed designer jeans and a Hard Rock

Cafe T-shirt, raising my hand in the traditional Indian salute.

"How," I intoned solemnly.

"What's shakin', Dude," he replied. "Looks like one of the bro's scalped you already."

I had forgotten these were *California* Indians.

I struck my chest. "My name Maxwell. What yours?"

The Indian looked at me strangely. "Just call me 'Ace.' What's on your mind?"

I was hoping it would be something more traditional, like "Tonto," but I let it pass. The main thing was that my Indian lingo was pretty good; I was getting through.

"Great White Father in Washington bring you greetings."

"You mean that dude who plays the sax?"

"Right. Great White Father say I can help you build big teepee where paleface tourists will pay much wampum to pitch pennies, play faro, fandango, and pull-tab games."

Aces eyes narrowed. "What's the split, dude?"

I felt sorry for this ignorant savage, who obviously knew nothing of high finance. Taking him would be child's play.

I struck my chest again and winced. This was starting to hurt. "Many expense for me," I said. "I take only ninety parts and give you ten."

"How'd you like to be fitted for an Arrow shirt, dude? We get the fat end of a 75-25 split of the gross, with a triple-net, back-load, lease-back production deal. *Capish?*"

I was beginning to suspect that this savage had been to Harvard Business School. I decided it best to humor him.

"We will smoke on it," I declared gravely.

"All *right*," said Ace. "You brought some pot?"

I quickly changed the subject. "What card games do you play here? Red dog? Faro?"

"Never hear of 'em," he replied. "My game's razz. Which

reminds me, who won the *World Series*. Damn *Card Player* never gets here in time. They must send it Pony Express."

Some of the Indians strolled over and Ace introduced them. They went by such names as "Bad Beat," "River Card," and "Double Belly-Buster." John Wayne would have fainted.

They liked my casino idea and asked about things like valet parking and a showroom. "Can we book Pee-Wee Herman?" Bad Beat asked. "Sure," said Double Belly-Buster. "Then he could deal double-exposure blackjack."

They asked what games we'd have and I mentioned stud, hold'em, Omaha high-low ... Suddenly the Bust-Outs went crazy, war-dancing and chanting. "Omaha HIGH-low, Omaha HIGH-low!"

I began to think these boys had been out in the sun too long. Talking about sun, I looked down and noticed my shoes were melting in the desert heat. I began to worry.

"How many tourists come here in the summer?" I asked.

The braves held a long powwow. "About six a month."

So ended my latest dream. And the last I saw of the Bust-Outs, they were hitchhiking down Interstate 15 to Vegas, still looking to raise enough for a buy-in.

# CONSULTING THE SPIRIT OF POKER

The more I play poker, the more I doubt the underlying mathematical order of the cosmos. When a superb player like me goes through a stack of chips faster than Big Denny goes through a stack of pancakes, when I'm running so bad that even my worst enemies like Action Al start smiling at me, it is during such moments of despair that I question Einstein's famous assurance that God does not play dice with the universe.

If not, he's playing roulette or *something*.

Poker pundit Mason Malmuth would probably tell me that my losses were falling within standard mathematical deviation. "America's Mad Genius," Mike Caro, would say that no one ever *runs* bad, but simply has *been* running bad. But I knew it had to be more than that!

Ignoring all reason, I became convinced that something was messing up my karma. Some demented, evil spirit was doing this to me. Darkly, I recalled the words of Hamlet: "There are more things in heaven and earth, Horatio, than are dreamt of in your philosophy."

Horatio lost his pants too, I bet.

Finally, my losing streak got me delirious enough to decide that Shirley MacLaine was right and that mysterious metaphysical forces really do rule our lives. Hoping she never read all the sarcastic things I wrote about her in the past, I found her phone number in the Yellow Pages under "New-Age Gurus" and made an appointment to have her check out my spiritual status.

When I met her, she asked my astrological sign; I told her it was Pisces. "Pisces," she nodded. "You are a fish. And what is your problem?"

"That *is* my problem," I replied.

She was trying to figure that out when she began staring at me. "I can see an aura rising from you," she whispered in awe.

"That's no aura," I told her. "That's cigarette smoke. I just spent ten hours in a card club."

"Tarot cards?"

"Poker cards," I explained. "A poker club is a place where you give money to the house so you can give money to other players."

"Enough of your gibberish," she snapped. "What wisdom do you seek of me?"

"I'm a top-drawer poker player," I blurted, "but lately I've been losing my a–, I mean my bankroll, something awful. No logical explanation. Gotta be spooks or something, and they say you can help."

"Perhaps. Are you familiar with channeling?"

*It says, "You are a fish."*

"I don't know. Is it anything like Omaha high-low?"

My spiritual guide squeezed her eyes shut and muttered something about sticking to theater and movies in the future. "Very well," she finally said, "I will summon the astral spirit of the 2,000-year-old poker warrior, On-Tilt.

"On-Tilt! On-Tilt!" she began chanting. "Before you comes a supplicant seeking your wise counsel."

The hairs on my arm (where else) stood on end as a deep and mysterious voice reverberated in the room: "Hey, Shirl, I told ya never to call me in the middle of a hand, ya know?"

"Forgive me, On-Tilt, but a worthy disciple named Max Shapiro seeks to know why his poker karma is being bent."

"Oh, that idiot," sneered On-Tilt. "Thou art being punished, fool, for mocking a fellow poker player in your writings. What hast Big Denny ever done to you?"

"He's threatened to sit on my head a couple of times."

"With good reason," proclaimed On-Tilt. "He deserves not thy cruel jests. Dost thou not believe that Big Denny is human, that he has a heart?"

"Not really, he ..."

"Silence!" thundered On-Tilt. "Swear now nevermore to defame this man, or thou will never again fill those inside straights thou loves to chase."

"OK, I promise. I'll find someone else to pick on. Is Ralph the Rattler OK?"

"Him you can slander all you want. I will fax the poker gods and have them remove the curse from your game."

"Oh, thank you, On-Tilt," I wept. "Does that mean I can start winning again?"

"No."

"No? You just promised to lift my curse."

"In truth. But you'll still be the same crappy player."

# SUE 'EM ALL

f you stay up all night playing poker as I do, you end up watching a lot of daytime television. That's because it's hard to sleep in the morning after pounding your head against the wall for calling three raises to chase the ignorant end of an inside straight with three spades and a pair on board the night before.

What fascinates me about the tube are the get-rich-quick commercials aired at all the low-lifes who watch daytime TV because they don't have jobs in the first place. Since I'm always vowing to give up poker in favor of a real job some day, I spent a lot of time watching the TV ads about new careers. You know: "Earn big money as a dental assistant!" "Become an embalmer in your spare time!" "Women look up to guys who drive those big 18-wheelers!" "Unlimited opportunities for deep-sea divers!" Then I found out you're supposed to pay *them* for going to their schools.

I also saw a lot of those attorneys who are only too eager to represent you in accident cases. They all look sincere, dressed in three-piece suits, posing in offices that are lined with shelves of law books — but they *all* have shifty eyes. My favorite injury commercial is the testimonial from the guy who brags about collecting four million bucks for being run over by a steamroller. Big deal. He's three inches tall now. What can he do with his money except go limbo dancing?

But lately these attorneys have been mining a new vein. Now they're going for deep-pocket employer lawsuits. You don't have to be cut in half in a sawmill accident to collect, either. On-the-job stress is all it takes. Suffer a headache or an upset stomach and you're set for life. Got some menial job like screwing in light bulbs? You deserve compensation for your low self-esteem! Boss yell at you for coming to work drunk? Sue him! Too many papers piled up on your desk? That's why you drink in the first place!

Since I wasn't getting anywhere on the career track, the lawyers got me thinking about all the abuse, indignities, pain, and suffering I've endured as a poker player. I even had a full head of hair when I started playing the game (of course, I was 12 years old at the time). So I called the Traumatized Workers, Slip-and-Fall, Drunk-Driving, and Undocumented-Aliens Legal Rights Defender Hot Line and made an appointment to see an attorney.

I decided to wear a nice suit and tie. Trouble is, my wardrobe consists mainly of shirts that say things like "El Centro Poker Room and Bowling Alley." Finally, in the back of the closet, I found a green polyester leisure suit I bought in 1976. Once I blew the dust off it didn't look too bad, even if it *was* too tight to button.

The attorney's office looked different from his impressive TV commercial, maybe because the office was a trailer parked behind a used car lot and the attorney was wearing a red polyester leisure suit too tight to button. "I'm a professional poker player," I told him. "I want to sue the card clubs and my editors who caused me trauma."

"You have come to the right place, my dear chap. Tell me what indignities you've been forced to endure."

I began weeping. "Everyone yells at me. Dealers scream at me for playing too slow or stealing chips, then they spit on me when I don't tip ... players laugh at me when I lose, and they throw cards at me when I win ... floormen always rule against me ... waitresses never get my order right ..." I paused to blow my nose. "And I hate the cursing," I continued, "especially when a nice little old lady is sitting at the table."

"How dreadful for them," said the legal rights defender.

"What I mean is, they use the worst words."

Then the attorney began weeping as I described how my trade forced me to associate with disreputable characters like Dirty Wally, Big Denny, and Ralph the Rattler.

"And how do your editors cause you injury?" he asked.

"They sometimes edit my columns."

The attorney smote his brow. "A *slam-dunk* case. We'll sue everyone for millions. Now we just have to verify that you're a professional player. How much did you make last year?"

I hesitated. "Counting my playing and everything?"

"Yes, yes, of course," he said impatiently.

"Well, I declared $1,500 on my tax return," I said.

"Come, come, my dear boy. We all know you poker professionals fudge a bit on your taxes. What did you *really* make last year?"

I bit my lip. "I lost $32,455.50. Lotta bad beats," I added helpfully.

"You blithering idiot! If you lost $32,000, why did you declare a profit on your taxes?"

"Professional pride," I responded haughtily.

"OK," said the attorney, trying to remain calm. "The IRS is satisfied you have a legitimate business if you just show a profit two years out of five. Surely you came out ahead two years out of five, didn't you? *Didn't you?*"

I stared out the window of the trailer for a long time. "Let's forget it," I finally said. "I think I'll go to deep-sea diving school after all."

# LUCKY CHARMS

One evening at the Commerce Casino we were treated to an amusing story by a congenial dealer named Bob. Bob said that he was standing at a stall in the men's room one night. All the other stalls were in use and a fellow was waiting behind him. Even when some stalls opened up, the guy still never moved. Bob got nervous and asked him what he was doing. The guy pointed and explained: "That's my lucky stall."

Everyone at our table laughed at the story, but I wondered if that guy was onto something. So I tracked him down and asked him how he picked a lucky urinal. He said ancient Chinese numerology was used to find lucky numbers for everything he did at the club: what space to park in, what food to order, and so on. I asked if this caused any problems. He said pushing other cars out of his lucky parking spot was hard work, but the worst thing was having to order the same item on the menu (No. 27), night after night after night. "Number 27 is fried okra," he screamed. I hate okra! It gives me gas."

I could have told him about a new strain of no-gas okra that agriculturists have developed called "okra windfree," but I wasn't interested in his problems.

He told me his lucky numbers had been figured out by a man named Lotsa Luck who owned an herb and potion shop called the "House of Much Fortune."

The next day I paid a visit to the shop. Lotsa Luck was a venerable old Oriental gentleman with most of his fingers missing. He said they had been bitten off by various lucky creatures that he had acquired for his potions. He also walked with a bad limp (the result of a lucky elephant stepping on his foot), and one ear had been blown off when a lucky potion he was brewing exploded. He also had a bandage on his head. A lucky ox skull had fallen off a shelf and knocked him cold the day before.

The first thing Lotsa Luck did was to cast my horoscope. The Chinese have a 12-year zodiac, with a particular animal ruling each sign. "You are a fish," he informed me — a bit of information I could have done without.

Then he told me my opposing and unlucky sign was the snake. "Stay away from snakes," he warned ominously.

Now he tells me! I've already got fang marks up and down both arms from playing against Ralph the Rattler. I analyzed my records one day and discovered that if the "Rattler" is just in the same club where I'm playing, I lose eighty percent of the time. Of course, I lose eighty percent of the time even when he's *not* there, but that's just coincidence.

I asked Lotsa Luck what he had in the way of lucky charms. He climbed up a ladder and reached for something. Just then the ladder broke and Lotsa Luck crashed to the floor. He screamed in pain and grabbed his arm, but otherwise pretended that nothing had happened.

He displayed a gold amulet and said it was guaranteed to bring good fortune to whoever possessed it. I asked him if anyone I heard of had ever worn it.

"You betcha," he beamed proudly. "Amelia Earhart."

I asked for something else. He reached under the counter, rapping his head smartly as he stood up. He opened a jar of ointment. "Rub on body. Brings very good luck, and also make you irresistible to ladies."

"Sounds good. Who's used it?"

"Mike Tyson."

"Forget it," I said.

"Shrinks hemorrhoids too," he added hopefully.

"Forget it! Hasn't *anybody* gotten anything from using your stuff?"

"You betcha. Zeek Malkovich. See his picture on television every week."

"Never heard of him."

"On 'Wide World of Sports.' Show him falling off ski jump."

Lotsa Luck named other famous clients like Leona Helmsley, Pete Rose, and the captain of the Titanic, but I was not impressed. I asked if any *poker players* had used his potions, and he pulled out a dusty old bottle filled with a noxious brown liquid.

"Wild Bill Hickok drank some, then got shot when he had aces and eights."

"You call that luck?"

"You betcha. It was a winning hand."

# FIGHTING WORDS

In terms of fights per hour, poker makes hockey seem as tame as a game of croquet at a country club ... or a convent. You sometimes wonder if you're in a cardroom or a biker bar.

Part of the problem is a lack of uniform rules. Every casino is a little duchy with laws unto itself. And not only do rules and interpretations differ from cardroom to cardroom, but sometimes from floorperson to floorperson as well. (Of course this problem is even worse at home games. Take Ralph the Rattler. He has rules posted on his wall, but they look as if they were written by a four year old. This is partly due to the Rattler's ignorance of grammar, but mostly it's so he can interpret any rule in his favor in a dispute. In fact, the *only* rule written in clear English is the one absolving the house of responsibility for bad checks.)

The other cause of fights is that most poker players are surly louts who would just as soon argue as play.

Other sports have a time-honored cry to signal the onset of action: "Play ball." "Gentlemen, start your engines." "The flag is up." "Shake hands and come out fighting." But in poker, any number of phrases can start action — and by action, I mean anything from an exchange of insults to flying chairs. Here then are some terms that can touch off a melee in any cardroom. Use them at your own peril.

*1. Lay your cards down; you've got a flush.* A guaranteed riot-maker. A player, thinking he has a loser, holds his cards in the air uncertainly; another player sees the hand and offers advice. *Never, never* do this, gentle reader. You may think you're being helpful, but believe me, the player you've cost the pot is legally entitled to kill you.

*2. You had a flush last hand.* This is a related incitement, just slightly less serious than the previously mentioned chain of events.

It occurs when a laid-down hand is overlooked by everyone in a confusing game like Omaha high-low. The victim will yell, "Why didn't you tell me then?" and the troublemaker will reply, "It wasn't my business." The victim will then demand the pot, to no avail, but it *will* stop the game for several acrimonious minutes.

*3. Can you please move your seat a little?* This sounds innocent enough, but I can guarantee the reply will be: "I'm sitting exactly where I'm supposed to be." This will lead to much sniping back and forth until a floorperson is called to rearrange the chairs, thus ticking off *everyone* at the table.

*4. Can you please move your ashtray?* This will result in the usual smoker/nonsmoker bickering ("If you can't stand smoke you shouldn't be here"). And if the ashtray *is* moved, then the player it gets closer to will start bitching.

*5. Gardena move.* This is an all-purpose insult rooted in the bad old days of dealerless poker in Gardena when sharpies would try to fake out other players with deceptive hand movements and misleading statements. If you want to provoke someone who just did something questionable (innocent or not), yell out "Gardena move!" and watch the sparks fly.

*6. The pot is short.* Try tossing that one out some time if you want to create mass confusion and hysteria.

*7. Change the deck.* This is always followed by another player's complaint: "It was just changed."

*8. Dealer, you mucked my hand!* When you hear this, you may as well go eat, because a 45-minute battle will follow. In sequence: A dealer erroneously pushes a winning hand into the discards. The victim yells bloody murder. The dealer fishes the hand out of the pile. He rules it a winner. The player who thought he won screams and refuses to give back the pot. It will take a floorman, his supervisor, and several security guards so long to straighten out this mess that the game can break up. And the decision can go any which way. Sometimes the player with the mucked hand gets the pot, sometimes not (for failure to protect his hand). If so, then sometimes the player who got beat suffers the loss, and sometimes the dealer has to come up with the extra chips.

*9. Short buy.* Normally I'm all sweetness and light, but this is one mischief-maker I cannot resist using against a certain old pest I detest. When he sits down, he digs an assortment of unmatched chips out of his pocket until he has the absolute minimum buy-in. I then yell, "Dealer, that man has a short buy! I want his chips counted down!" The dealer is forced to make this demeaning count, and I beam in ecstasy as the furious old pest nearly has apoplexy cursing and rattling his teeth at me. (Of all the things that give me the most pleasure in life, this must surely rank in the top ten.)

*10. I want to see those cards.* Someone has just taken a monster bad beat in a monster pot. He's sitting there with steam coming out of his ears, when some clod demands that his cards be turned over. The clod could have several motives for doing this — all of them irksome. He could be suggesting that the loser is playing partners with the winner and was raising on nothing. He could be trying to gain information on how the guy plays. Or he could be trying to needle him by asking, "What kind of hand could that idiot possibly have?" Usually, the bad-beatee will respond to this request by saying, "Sure," and then savagely bury his hand in the discards. Now the fight is on for real.

*11. I already asked for that seat.* Player A gets up to move to a vacated "lucky" seat, when Player B says he already staked his claim. If the dealer to whom this alleged prior request was made is no longer at the table, a protracted verbal and possibly physical tug of war may ensue.

*12. How could you possibly play that hand?* (See example No. 10.) When a loser in a big pot has turned over his cards and is staring in dismay at his second-best hand, those are the *last* words he wants to hear. And sometimes those *will* be the last words the smart aleck will get to utter.

*13. String raise!* If a player makes a "two-part" raise by reaching back for more chips, an opponent can use this term to nullify the raise. But sometimes the raiser argues that he also verbally announced a raise. What happens then is that two players will concede he mumbled something but they didn't hear what it was, another will claim he really said "Call," a couple more will insist he didn't say anything, and a player who wants to reraise will testify he heard a raise declared as clear as a bell. If lie detector tests were administered, *everyone* at the table would flunk.

*14. Quit letting that guy see your cards!* This is a nice double-barreled insult. You're accusing one player of ineptly flashing cards and another of unethically peeking at them. The alternative and even nastier implication is that both players are in collusion.

*15. Would you like to buy some chips?* A very subtle insult. When a player with a ton of chips offers to sell some to an opponent who is very low on chips, it appears that he is just trying to be helpful. But what he's *really* saying is, "I'm a big winner, and the way you play, you're sure to lose the few chips you have left, so you'd better rebuy now."

*16. You fouled my hand!* This is a very explosive situation. It occurs when some neurotic sore loser throws his cards and they land on your live hand. The closest I ever came to climbing over the table and throttling a player occurred when some drunk did this to me, and when I glared at him, he muttered that I should have protected my cards with a chip.

*17. Hey, I didn't check!* Who can count how many fights these words have triggered? This situation happens when several players have checked after another player, who then suddenly comes to life and yells that he never passed. He may have made some innocent motion that was interpreted as a check, he might have been bypassed while he was daydreaming or studying his cards, or he might even have made a "move," hoping he could either check-raise or call back the action if nobody bet.

*18. Table change.* A request to jump ship is a general slur on the entire table. Except everyone thinks that *he* is the good guy and that it's the others who are rocks or jerks. But when the escapee is a little more specific, pointing at you and growling, "Table change — get me *away* from this creep," you know for whom the fight bell tolls: It tolls for thee.

*19. I never agreed to split a jackpot with you!* I have saved the worst for last. These are the most chilling words you will ever hear at a table. They will do more than start a fight; they will set off a war, a lifelong vendetta that will turn best friends into mortal enemies. And this is the best reason I can offer for beating off with a stick any stranger who suggests a friendly little jackpot split. Besides, the chances are that the guy already has sold twenty-five percent of himself to 50 other people, and if by some miracle he did hit a jackpot, he'd throw his hand away.

# AND THE LOSERS SAY, 'DEAL'

**T**he adage about nothing being certain but death and taxes should be revised, because there is one additional absolute in this otherwise unpredictable world we live in — *Any home poker game will always end in a dispute over quitting time.*

Getting eight or nine poker players to agree on — and stick to — a quitting time is like getting a unanimous verdict from jurors in the O.J. Simpson or Menendez brothers trials. Working out a Bosnian peace agreement to the satisfaction of everyone would be a snap by comparison. The only way a home game can ever end harmoniously at the appointed hour would be if every player is exactly even at the precise moment that quitting time rolls around.

Take the player who finds himself a ton ahead an hour before games end. "My last hand, boys," he'll announce abruptly. "I've got an early morning business meeting tomorrow." Now, the only time in his life this bum ever got out of bed before lunch was the time he was thrown out by the 6.6 Northridge earthquake, and the only meeting he ever attended was with his parole board. But let him get a hundred bucks ahead and suddenly he's turned into a model of discipline and punctuality.

On the other hand, consider the player who places his hand on his breast at the beginning of the game and solemnly declares, "Win, lose, or draw, tonight I'm leaving at ten sharp. I don't care if it's in the middle of a hand. I'm having open-heart surgery at seven tomorrow morning."

Need I bother to explain what happens next? As we all know,

come the appointed hour, he'll be stuck like a pig, studiously avoiding eye contact with the other players or the clock. And the conversation will go:

Another player: "It's past your quitting time, Jerry."

Silence.

"You said you would die if you played late."

"Deal."

"But what about your surgery ..."

"Don't worry about my bleepin' surgery! Just shut up and deal the bleepin' cards!"

Every home game becomes a predictable vaudeville routine as quitting time nears. The winners are making extended trips to the bathroom. They're counting down their chips, yawning, and looking

at their watches. If the host is ahead, he'll be busy tidying up the kitchen. Meanwhile, the losers are wild-eyed, sweating, and breathing hard. They're urging everyone to play faster and pleading for some sort of negotiated extension.

"How about another hour, guys? Two more rounds? One more hand?"

The winners all have busy schedules the next day and the losers are arguing that tomorrow isn't important.

"Hey, we can sleep late tomorrow, it's a holiday."

"What holiday?"

"Uh ...Valentine's Day, isn't it?"

I've tried to find a solution to this problem. I thought of licensing home games the same as bars; anyone serving cards past quitting time has his license revoked. I considered having each player post a forfeiture bond for quitting early or trying to play late. I even wondered about a time-release lock for the door. But even these fantasy solutions wouldn't do any good because, like leading a horse to water, you can get a big winner to stay, but you can't make him play.

Take this guy I know named Harvey. Once he gets ahead his usual two grand, he sits there with his arms folded so tightly that gangrene sets in. You realize you're not going to get any of your chips back from him when he goes to the fireplace and returns with a stack of logs to sit behind.

So the winning rocks will play only locks, while the steaming losers get deeper in hock. But, like Oliver Twist begging for more gruel ("Please, sir, I want more"), this never stops them from optimistically begging for "just one more round." That sage philosopher, Yogi Berra, once observed of baseball, "The game isn't over till it's over." Now here is Shapiro's quotation for a home poker game:

"The game isn't over till at least two rounds after it's supposed to be over."

# THE IRS RAKES THE POT

The Internal Revenue Service has caught the scent of blood and is going after the poor jackpot player. Clubs have been informed by the tax collector that they must withhold twenty percent of payouts for federal taxes.

Like the fisherman with his prize marlin in *The Old Man and the Sea,* you may fight off the smaller fish, but you won't escape that killer shark.

I discovered this when I hit the small end of a jackpot worth a cool $1,250. "I'm set for life," I thought. A second later I was being circled by predators. Action Al tugged on my sleeve to beg a small loan. Someone else asked me to return the money I owed *him.* The dealer, floorperson, cocktail waitress, and three porters all stuck out their hands, and some guy with a "Will work for food or buy-in," cardboard sign rushed in off the street.

Tearing Action Al's hand away, I made a break for it as the pack bayed and nipped at my heels. Bursting into the casino office, I asked for my $1,250 and an armed escort. I got only a grand. The feds had hit me even before Action Al.

This was an outrage. Next morning I stormed into the local IRS office, determined to fight this injustice. "No taxation without representation!" I shouted.

"Sorry," an IRS agent yawned. "Winnings are taxable."

"It isn't winnings," I argued. "It's return of capital." The agent fell to the floor laughing — but I pressed on. "They drop two bucks a hand in the $5-$10 game," I explained. That's about twenty-five cents a player and they deal about thirty hands an hour, so it costs me $7.50 each hour. I average thirty hours a week, which means in eight years I've paid out $93,600 in jackpot collections. I finally get $1,250 of it back, and you want me to pay tax?"

"Can you document all that playing time?"

"Take a look at this," I said, handing him a photograph.

The agent studied the evidence. "Looks like two charbroiled steaks," he observed.

"That's an X-ray of my lungs. They've turned black from all the secondhand smoke I've had to inhale in eight years."

"Insufficient," ruled the IRS man. "Next time get a receipt each time you're dealt a hand."

"Then how about deducting my tips?" I persisted. "I toked the dealer $300."

"How much?"

"Would you believe $125?"

"*How much,* Mr. Shapiro?"

"OK, I slipped him ten bucks. But I also bought the floorperson a Coke."

"Very well," sighed the tax man. "We'll allow you $10.50 for deductions. Anything else?"

"Yeah, I made a twenty-five percent jackpot split deal with Benny."

"And just who is 'Benny?'" the agent inquired.

"Everyone knows Benny. He's a great guy. We're best friends. Phone him ... he'll tell you I split with him."

The agent dialed the number I gave him, and after ten rings he was greeted with a surly grunt. I had forgotten it was only 9 a.m. and Benny never got up before noon.

"I have a gentleman in my office who claims he gave you twenty-five percent of his jackpot," the tax man said.

"Please inform me as to the name of the individual who is telling you this nonsense," Benny requested.

"A Mr. Max Shapiro. He says he's your best friend."

"Never heard of him."

"He says he has pictures of the two of you together at the Miss Nude USA beauty pageant in Barstow."

"Oh, *that* Max Shapiro. Well, I certainly would never trust *him* to split a jackpot."

"Don't do this to me, Benny," I screamed. "They're liable to throw me in jail."

"Good. Maybe you can pick up some new material there. Your articles have been very weak lately."

I put my head on the desk and began to sob. The agent took pity. "Look," he said, "maybe you can deduct some expenses. Like mileage for driving to the club."

"Of course," I sniffled. "It's thirty miles round trip and it costs me five dollars per mile to drive.

"A car doesn't cost five dollars a mile to drive."

"It does if it's a car that Benny sold you."

"Well, I wouldn't worry too much," said the agent. "I looked up your returns for prior years. Even with this $1,250 income, you'll still be below the poverty level."

"You mean I'll get back my $250 when I file my return?"

"Not quite," he said. "We use the same jackpot accounting system as the casinos."

"Which means ... ?"

"Which means you'll get back your ten-dollar tip."

# POKER PESTS

ike bugs and beasties at a picnic, poker pests come in endless number — and in every conceivable variety. A subject that never will be exhausted, these players aggravate me so much that they cause the same facial tics that Inspector Clouseau caused his boss in the *Pink Panther* movies. It's painful to write about, but at least it's cheaper than talking to a shrink.

Some are like lady bugs. They're harmless and can even benefit mankind. Take *rabbit hunters,* for example. There are occasions when I'd like to see the last card too, so I don't mind them very much.

But others are irritants, like ticks that do nothing but spread disease. Take players who call for a new deck every round and a new set-up every hour. They merely slow the action — annoying in a rake game and infuriating at a time-collection table.

The nonstop talkers to me are like flies, endlessly buzzing around you. They comment on every hand being played and rehash every hand when it's over.

Even worse are the coffee-housers who speak with forked tongue. They're like snakes trying to get you off your guard with their cunning lies and their slithery insinuations.

Or the snails ... the players who don't pick up their cards until the action gets to them and then they stare at them blankly forever. And with each round, they have to recheck their hole cards, either because they've forgotten what they were, or to make sure they haven't changed.

To punish these pests, I'd like to borrow an idea from Colonial days. Back then, petty offenders like scolds and gossips would be locked in wood frame devices called stocks and put on display in the town square. Signs around their necks spelled out their offenses, and the townsfolk had a jolly old time ragging them.

Now, I readily admit that some of my grievances are irrational, but that's my business. And perhaps my own behavior or appearance causes as much pain to my fellow players as theirs does to me. I certainly hope so. Anyway, here are more things I can do without:

*The amnesiacs:* These are the simple souls whose minds are out for space walks and who require a wake-up call from the dealer whenever it's their turn to act. While in the stocks, an amnesiac should be slapped and doused with ice water at regular intervals, while someone yells in his ear: "It's on you, Clyde!"

*People with cellular phones ...* to show everyone how important they are, no doubt. Hey, this is a poker table, not an office. If you want to make a call, use one of the poker room's phones. And the way electronic gear keeps shrinking, before long I expect these people to start bringing not only their own phone, but a computer, fax, and copy machine to the table.

*The happy wanderers:* These are the "mark me absent" pests who continually play one round and disappear for three. They could be anywhere — checking tournament action, in the bar, in the TV room. But more often than not, they're playing a few hands at the pai gow table. These escape artists should be fitted with a ball and chain to slow them down or an electronic collar to make them easy to locate.

*People who clutter the table with their lucky charms ...* rabbit's feet, horseshoes, figurines, you name it. Not only do I abhor such ignorant superstition, it drains the luck away from my side of the table.

*The inexperts:* We're all familiar with the "experts" who

criticize anyone who wins with an unlikely hand. But what sets my teeth on edge is when some boor yells at me, "How could you play that hand?" when I know my strategy was correct. If this happens to you, don't bother to justify your play. Just try to infuriate the lout even more by chirping, "I had a feeling," or something equally inane. (Incidentally, this happens to me even more at blackjack. Please, people, quit informing me that I already had an eighteen made when I hit a soft eighteen against a dealer's nine or ten. I *know* what I'm doing. One time I made the correct play of splitting sixes against a dealer's five, and a loudmouthed woman stood up and indignantly proclaimed she would not play at the same table with someone as incompetent as me.)

*People who make noise while eating their food* ... marginally bearable at the clubs where the background din at least helps mask all the slurping and lip smacking. Unfortunately, I also play in a home game where two players with the social graces of starving dogs make my stomach do roller coaster drops every Tuesday night.

*The cushion hogs:* It really chaps my hide when I can't find a spare cush for my sore tush, and then I spot someone sitting on four of them (plus two behind his back) looking as if he just had hemorrhoid surgery. He's sitting so high his nose is bleeding. For punishment, make these hoarders sit on rocks in the stocks.

*People who keep telling me what they would have made if they had played the hand* ... invariably, these *nudniks* sit on the side of my bad ear. I have no idea what they're trying to say, and all night long I just keep nodding my head up and down in feigned understanding like those stupid bobbing dogs that people, for some reason or other, put in the rear windows of their cars. My head nodding stopped, however, the night I realized I was nodding to a guy who was asking me to loan him fifty bucks.

*The vulgarians:* Obscenities make me squirm when women

are at the table. Players who wouldn't dream of using bad words in front of their mothers think nothing of unleashing a stream of them in front of someone else's mother — or grandmother. How I'd love to see these foul mouths put on display in the stocks while their mouths were washed out with soap.

*People with false teeth who rattle and click them all night long* ... if I want castanets, I'll go to a Spanish nightclub.

*"Russian" dealers:* I must include dealers in one category of my personal pest list, but this has nothing to do with ethnicity. I'm talking about dealers who are always rushin' you to act. Speeding up the game (and tokes) is one thing. It's quite another when they repeatedly hit the table, point at me, and nag, "On you, sir," a split second after a card is dealt. They're like drivers who blow their horns behind you the instant a light turns green. On more than one occasion, I've gone absolutely berserk and screamed at the dealer, "I *know* it's on me! I *always* know when it's on me! Just deal and shut @*$ up!" (Yes, I know what I said about cussing at the table, but there are times when it's justified.)

*Cigar smokers:* Let's see, what unwelcome-at-a-picnic creature can I compare them to without getting into too much trouble? Well, you've got this cute little black furry animal with a white stripe who sometimes lifts his tail and ...

*People who smoke and drop ashes on everything* ... the table, the floor, the chair, themselves — everything but the ashtray. The worst ash-dropper I ever saw was a card club habitué affectionately known to one and all as "Crazy Eddie." When Crazy Eddie left the table, they had to bring in a cleaning crew to repair the damage. I used to watch the ash on his cigarette grow ever longer and silently prayed it would drop in his crotch and set him on fire. I had to be careful of what I said to him, however, because Crazy Eddie was dangerously deranged. He once got barred from a club for pulling a knife on someone who welshed on a backgammon bet. It's safe to talk about him now, though, because a while back Crazy Eddie croaked of a heart attack in the men's room of his favorite card club. If I ever happen to look up and see ashes raining down from heaven, I'll know where they're coming from.

*The floorwalkers* ... characters I always see walking back and forth between the tables at one club or another. They're *always* there. They never play. They rarely speak to anyone. They just walk, back and forth, side to side, like sentries on duty. Who are they? What do they want? When do they sleep? Are they with the IRS? Does someone pay them to stroll around? To me, this is a mystery larger than the Sphinx, and some day I plan to solve it.

*People who read my articles at the table without laughing* ... idiots. Want me to explain the jokes to you?

*People who ask me if I actually get paid for what I write* ... oh, of course not, I pay the magazine!

*The ultimate pest:* The animal that gets my vote as the most obnoxious pest of all is ... the envelope please ... the card thrower. In fact, the only person I can think of who's lower than a card thrower is someone who not only throws cards, but does so out of turn.

This is the one character who is held in my lowest esteem. This is the baby who never got properly potty trained, the infant who flung his porridge off his high chair, the spoiled child who always got what he wanted from mommy if he cried long and loud enough.

Didn't make your flush on the end? Wham! Got outdrawn by a chaser with no business in the pot? Whop! Lost two hands in a row? Whoosh! Out sail the cards in *every* direction — toward the dealer, toward other players, straight up, on the floor. Not infrequently, they're thrown hard enough to cause injury. Even worse, they can land on your cards and foul your hand.

And each time one of these infantile monsters throws a tantrum, your blood pressure and the level of tension at the table rise a notch.

To me, these players are like ants, flies, spiders, snakes, and a thunderstorm all hitting your picnic simultaneously.

Occasionally a dealer will be bold enough to ask the player to refrain from throwing cards. Once in a while, a floorperson will be called over if the player ignores the dealer. And once in a blue moon, if the player does not obey the floorperson, he may *actually* be ejected.

But one can't always depend on management for protection. Instead, I have a proposal for those of us civilized and genteel enough to abhor the practice of card throwing. Let's take the law into our own hands and go after these varmints vigilante-style.

Give them a taste of their own medicine. When someone throws cards, pick them up and throw them right back at him (or her). If you can't reach the cards throw a newspaper. Throw food, ashtrays, dinner plates, lighted cigarettes, chairs — whatever is handy. Even better, set up an area for public punishment of these miscreants. You know that carnival attraction where the clown sticks his head through a hole in the canvas and you throw baseballs at him? Wouldn't that be lovely — and fitting.

And in the event that any of you card throwers are reading this, I offer this advice. Come on, ladies and gents, it's only a game. Lighten up. You'll play better and you won't spoil things for the rest of us.

# HEARD ANY GOOD LIES LATELY?

f Pinnochio played poker, his nose by now would be too long to fit inside a cardroom. If Diogenes took his lantern to look for a truthful poker player, he'd use up so much lantern fuel that the price of crude oil would be boosted back to thirty dollars a barrel.

Deception and poker just go hand-in-hand, like ham and eggs. So, as a service to any innocent readers who haven't discovered this yet, I'd like to present some expressions commonly heard around poker tables, explaining what they *seem* to mean versus what they *really* mean.

• "Somebody bet?"

*What it's supposed to mean:* "Somebody has a hand strong enough to bet? I'll have to think about this."

*What it really means:* "I can't believe some fool bet into my powerhouse. What I have to think about is whether to slow-play with a crying call or raise that sucker."

• "Lemme raise just in case you're bluffing."

*What it's supposed to mean:* "I have a fair hand so I'm going to test you with a raise."

*What it really means:* "I hope you really do have a strong hand because I can beat anything you have."

• "Pair the board!" (This is often heard in hold'em when there are three suited cards in the flop.)

*What it's supposed to mean:* "I have trips and I need to fill up to beat the flush that somebody holds."

*What it really means:* "I've got the nut flush made and if the dealer *does* pair the board to fill somebody's unfinished house he'll never see a tip from me again."

• "I'm not winning. I bought in for a thousand." (This is the automatic wail of a player to the friend who stops by the table and admires the mounds of chips he has all over the place.

*What it's supposed to mean:* "Don't be fooled by appearances because I'm really stuck like a pig."

*What it really means:* "I never had a thousand dollars at one time in my entire life. I bought in for one stack and these are all winnings along with the couple of white chips I sneaked into my pocket. But if you think I'm going to lend *you* anything, you're crazy."

• "I'm not playing tight ... I just haven't been getting any cards." (This is the standard response of an old rock who's being harassed by other players.)

*What it's supposed to mean:* "I'm *trying* to play loose, but

*"I hope you really do have a strong hand because I can beat anything you have."*

the cards have been terrible."

*What it really means:* "I haven't been dealt a pat six in the past hour."

• "I'm just a lucky player." (The usual explanation from the resident shark in a home game who's won nineteen times in a row.)

*What it's supposed to mean:* "Poker is a game of luck. You guys are as good as me, but I've just been catching cards."

*What it really means:* "Lucky? I've got a Ph.D. in poker. If I ever lost to you pigeons I'd take the cards to a testing laboratory."

• "I'm not going to bet into a flop like that!" (Typical comment in hold'em when the flop comes queen-jack-ten suited.)

*What it's supposed to mean:* "I've got a high pair but I'd be crazy to bet into a straight or flush."

*What it really means:* "I've got a royal flush and I'm not going to give my hand away. Let some other sucker bet it."

• "I'll have to squeeze this card real careful to see if I caught a spade."

*What it's supposed to mean:* "I hope I made my flush draw."

*What it really means:* "What would I want with a spade? I went in with three kings and a kicker."

• "King-high straight."

That's what you say when a player asks you what you had when he doesn't call your pure bluff.

• "Nothing."

That's what you say when you have a full house and a player asks what you had after he throws his hand away.

The above sampling is by no means exhaustive, but provides a good representative guide. Actually, the real problem doesn't come from the player who tries to spread misinformation. You expect that. What you have to watch out for is the sneak who tells you the truth.

# POKER AXIOMS

Some poker probabilities, such as the chances of making a flush draw, can be determined with mathematical precision. Others, while not lending themselves to such precise calculations, seem to come to pass so very frequently that they become givens, or self-evident axioms.

The best example of a sure-fire prediction involves dropping a piece of buttered toast on the kitchen floor. Everyone knows it will *always* land buttered side down.

Poker is replete with these same truisms. By way of example, I would like to list twenty five of these self-evident axioms, which henceforth will be known as "Max's Axioms."

1. A cold seat will catch fire the first hand after you abandon it.
2. A player who says "Let's gamble" is holding the nuts.
3. Misdeals occur only when you hold a premium hand.
4. If two players drive to a club together, one will insist on leaving just when the other is stuck like a pig and starting to come back.
5. The one time in your life you are dealt a pat royal flush, no one will call.
6. When a dealer sits down and greets the players with a hearty, "How's everyone doing today?" no one will bother to reply.
7. Drunks are always lucky, and the drunker they are, the luckier they are.
8. If you are paged for a phone call, inevitably it will be while you are pondering a tough call in a monster pot.
9. The moment you win your first hand in three hours, someone will call for a deck change.
10. Any mistake made by a dealer will always be to the other players' advantage and to your detriment.

11. When you make a smart laydown against a player who bluffs only one day a year, this will be the day of the year he has decided to bluff.

12. When you make an even smarter laydown against a player who never bluffs, he will have misread his hand and hold absolutely nothing.

13. No matter how rotten the game you are currently playing is, when you ask for a table change, the floorperson will manage to put you into an even worse one.

14. The night you bring your girlfriend to the cardroom (so you can show off while she watches you play) is the night you will suffer your all-time worst loss.

15. If you are two minutes late getting back from a meal break, your chips will be picked up.

16. If another player is missing for hours, he won't be picked up until the table starts to riot. And then the inconsiderate oaf will get back just in time to reclaim his seat.

17. When you promise yourself you will play "just one more hand" and then get up, you will always find a good reason to break your word to yourself.

18. If you are called for a new game and pick up your chips to change tables, the new game will never go. And by the time you rush back to your old table, your seat will have been filled.

19. Whenever you limp in with a weak hand you know you shouldn't be playing, someone will raise.

20. If you're a non-smoker and you forget to bring your fan, you will end up seated between two chain smokers.

21. If you're coming down with a cold, you will be seated directly under the Arctic blast of an air conditioning vent.

22. When you're smarting over a monumental bad beat, someone will always ask to see your hand.

23. The more chips you are carrying to the cashier's window, the more likely you are to run into a mooch.
24. A conservative player always thinks of himself as "solid" and is convinced that everyone who plays the same way he does is "tight."
25. At the showdown, if you turn up your hand before you are required to, you'll end up being slow-rolled by the player who should have acted first, but hesitated.

As a bonus, I would like to add my own personal Max's axiom.

If I go down to a club to pick up a magazine that features one of my articles, I will end up playing "as long as I'm here." And when I do, I will end up losing several times as much as I was paid for the article.

No other job in the world comes with such an occupational hazard.

# POKER GAME MUTATIONS

**P**oker is unique because it can mutate itself into different forms ... like a virus. In this spirit, I have created several new poker games guaranteed to generate excitement.

These games are fully protected under copyright laws of the United States, the British Commonwealth, and all other countries of the Berne and Universal Copyright Conventions including Patagonia and Lapland. For permission to play any game, send a quarter and a box of Cracker Jacks (prize included) to the author in care of the publishing company suspect enough to produce this book.

*Ahamo:* Astute readers will notice that Ahamo is Omaha spelled backwards. The chief complaint about Omaha is that it is a river-card game with the last card a nutcracker that turns nut hands into broken shells.

Ahamo cures this problem by being dealt *backwards.* The fifth-street card is the first board card to be dealt. This completely eliminates any nasty surprises. The fourth-street card is dealt next, and finally the flop. This is a much more civilized version of the game.

*Penguin:* This game is identical to panguigne, the only difference being that it is played with penguins. Each time a player wins a hand he pulls a feather from the bird. When the penguin is completely plucked the player with the most feathers gets to take the bird home for dinner. In case the penguin has had his dinner already, you can take him to a movie

*Mediocrity:* I predict real popularity for this game. At present, there are two categories of poker — high (the best hand wins)

and low (the worst hand takes down the money). The problem is that it's not easy to make the very best hands. It's tough to make a wheel and much harder to make a royal flush. The vast majority of players are average and they make average or mediocre hands. In the game mediocrity, the most mediocre hand is the winning hand. In draw poker, for example, the average winning hand for high is jacks and fours. The average winning hand for low is 8-5-4-2-A. Those are your *best* hands in mediocrity. From there, hands drop equally in value up or down. Therefore, jacks and threes would be equal to jacks and fives. An 8-5-3-2-A would have the same rank as 8-5-4-3-A. Some day, I anticipate a World Series of Mediocrity.

*Two-Card Stud:* Asian poker is a stripped-deck, five-card stud game with flushes beating full houses. Its sudden popularity signals a trend toward streamlined poker that will achieve its ultimate form in two-card stud. This game may be played with up to nine players. It uses eight cards — 2-4-6-8-10-K-A — in varying suits. Each player is dealt two cards face up, but the players are not allowed to look at them. A pair is the highest possible hand, followed by a full house, a flush, three-of-a-kind, and a straight flush. Each time a player gets a card, it is customary to pound the table and exclaim, "Herring, herring," though no one has determined why.

*Ladies Poker:* I get a lot of mail from feminists who think that having just one ladies-only event in tournaments is insufficient — they want their own game. Since I have had my consciousness raised by Shirley MacLaine, I am sympathetic to their needs and have devised this format.

First, they get their own deck of cards. The chauvinistic jacks and kings with their ugly whiskers and brutal swords and axes are instead all-female court cards: queens, princesses, and duchesses. The likenesses are of feminine icons such as Leona

Helmsley, Imelda Marcos, Tammy Faye Bakker, and Zsa Zsa Gabor. Instead of weapons of war, they will hold more appropriate symbols. For example, Imelda will hold a shoe, Zsa Zsa a summons.

The suits are hearts, diamonds, pearls, and roses. Stakes will not exceed a half-dollar, and each game will have eight wild cards. Players are supportive at all times. No nasty check-raising allowed. When a woman wins a pot, she doesn't snarl, "Get if fixed, sucker." She instead tries to soothe her opponent: "Don't cry, dear. You played that hand very well." The only table talk allowed is gossip and when the game breaks up, all the losers get their money back while the women chat over coffee and diet cheesecake.

# THE TIGHTEST PLAYER IN THE WORLD

I recently had the pleasure of interviewing Aberdeen Angus McTavish, the current national poker champion of Scotland, which of course makes him the tightest player in the world.

How tight are Scottish poker players? Well, the championship hold'em game lasted twelve days because the two finalists refused to play anything less than aces. The stand-off finally ended when Aberdeen Angus and Edinburgh Eddie McNeil both were dealt bullets; then four spades hit the board to give Angus a winning flush and the title.

"Ach, I should have been morrr patient and waited till I had better aces," Edinburgh Eddie lamented afterward. "But just as well, since the cows sore needed milkin' by then."

It sounded like an interesting story. So when I read that Angus had flown to the States (economy class, of course) to promote his new poker book, and would be in town for a book-signing, I went to the store where he was appearing.

There he was, a ruddy-cheeked man in kilts and a plaid Stetson, signing his name in the teeniest script I had ever seen. (I later learned that all Scotsmen write that way to conserve ink.) I asked if I could interview him.

"Canna ye not see that I'm busy, lad?" he burred.

"I'll buy you lunch," I offered.

Angus whipped out a sign that read, "Back in forty-five minutes," grabbed my arm, and bustled me out the door. "Ask me anything, laddie," he beamed.

We found a nice restaurant down the street. When we walked

in, Angus grabbed half the after-dinner mints off the counter and stuffed them in his pocket. Then, after making sure I would pick up the tab, he ordered a porterhouse steak and single-malt scotch. When he was finished eating and into his third scotch, I asked him to describe his book.

"It says, 'Play tight,'" he said.

"Is that the gist of the text?"

"Aye, and 'tis also the whole of the text — just the two words: 'Play tight.'"

"Wait a minute," I protested. "You can't write a book with just two words."

"We Scots are very thrrrifty with our words," he replied. "In any event, I got the idea from Roy West. All he ever writes in his articles is 'Play happy.'"

Angus ordered another single malt. His tab had already far exceeded what I'd get paid for the interview so I decided I'd better talk faster.

"What's your favorite hand?" I asked.

"A suited ace," Angus replied.

"Suited with what?"

"Anotherrr ace, of course."

"Don't you ever play anything but aces?" I persisted.

Angus pondered at some length. "Kings — if there's been no rrraise." He thought some more. "Perhaps queens, if I'm on the button." Suddenly he frowned and his face reddened. "Once I played a pairrr of jacks in early position. Of course, I was a wee bit drrrunk at the time."

"Doesn't sound like Scottish poker has much action," I commented.

"Aye. A hand once came up in a tournament and there were thrrree callers. Made all the front pages. Biggest news since Sandy McTeague's cow gave birth to a two-headed calf."

"I heard your prize amounted to five thousand pounds," I said. "May I ask how much you tipped the dealers?"

Aberdeen Angus suddenly experienced a violent coughing fit and pretended he didn't hear the question.

It was becoming plain that the man was as tight as two coats of paint; he was even helping himself to sugar packets off nearby tables. Tiring of his miserliness, I tried to change the subject.

"What do you think of the new four-color decks?" I asked.

"We've had them in Scotland for yearrrs," he shrugged. "Sometimes six-color, even eight-color decks."

"How can you have eight colors in a four-suited deck?"

"Oh, the suits haven't changed, laddie; 'tis the backs that have different colors. In Scotland we neverrr throw decks out; we mix them together when cards get torn."

As we walked out (with Angus taking the remaining after-dinner mints), I asked him how book sales were going.

"Excellent, laddie. I'm even working on a sequel."

"Do you have a title?"

"Aye. 'Play Tight — With Good Position.'"

# SECTION TWO

# But Poker's Real ...

... Poker is not primarily a game of luck. It is a game of skill.
*David Sklansky*

Poker is a game that pits your skill against your opponents' luck.
*Max Shapiro*

# FISHING FOR SUCKERS WITH FRESH-AIR FREDDY

**M**y friend Fresh-Air Freddy is always after me to do healthy things with him, like deep-sea fishing. "Think about breathing in all that clean salt air."

I told him that after years of inhaling cardroom smoke, I didn't think my lungs could handle the pure stuff, and the only fish I wanted to reel in were at the poker table.

"Hey, man," Fresh-Air Freddy said. "They play poker on the fishing boat."

I was intrigued. My mind flashed on all those legendary shipboard gambling settings: Mississippi riverboats where plantations were bet on the turn of a card; luxury ocean liners plied by cardsharps in dinner jackets; World War II troop ships where GIs gambled wildly for money they might not live to spend.

"What stakes do they play for?"

"Ten and twenty, I think," Freddy replied slyly.

Not bad, I thought. A guy could make a nice hit on one of those boats. I decided I should look the part of a real fisherman and told Freddy to write down what I'd need.

The tab for a rod and reel and line and sinkers and lures and hooks and floats and tackle box and license and boat ticket and a lot more came to more than two bills. A good investment, I kept reminding myself. Freddy said I could get lucky and hit the jackpot.

"They play jackpot poker?" I yelled in excitement.

"Ha, ha. What a character," said Freddy. That was his favorite expression. In fact, it was his only expression. "The jackpot is for catching the biggest fish."

We got to Oxnard around 11 p.m. for the overnight trip. The boat was the Pacific Queen, but it looked a lot smaller than it sounded. "Is that thing safe?" I asked.

"Splendid vessel," said Freddy. "Let's get on board and get some sleep."

I stumbled on deck with all my gear, then followed Freddy down a narrow passage to a small cubicle packed with fishermen. It looked like the hold of a slave ship. I somehow managed to climb up to a top bunk, cracked my head on the ceiling, and as the engines revved up and the boat started rocking, I started to wonder what I was doing here.

After a fitful night's sleep dreaming of being eaten by sharks, I woke to feel the Pacific Queen lurching and rolling through sickening swells. I staggered up on deck to confront a bleak vista of nothing but cold gray water surrounded by cold gray sky. I understood why Christopher Columbus' men wanted to turn back.

Fresh-Air Freddy was on deck breathing deeply and hooking up a fishing rig. "When do we play poker?" I asked.

"Ha, ha. What a character. On the way back. How about some breakfast?"

I turned pale and shook my head. After a while the boat stopped and fishermen crowded elbow to elbow along the rail. I managed to put a hook into a live anchovy bait and cast my line out with a mighty heave.

It traveled five feet, then my reel jammed and the line tangled fiendishly. I tried unsuccessfully to undo all the knots, then gave up and cut about fifty feet off my filament. On my second cast I managed to get entangled with three angry fishermen. One of them cut my line free. There went another fifty feet — plus tackle. The third time I just let the sinker drop straight down; something ferocious hit the bait and my reel whizzed. I began battling the monster. Must be the world's biggest albacore, I thought, Maybe a tuna. Or a marlin! I began winning the fight, and finally a huge, dark gray shape broke the surface.

"Get a gaff! A net! A winch," I screamed.

A deckhand appeared. "That's a shark. Can't get those things on the boat." He cut my line.

After about four hours, I managed to catch a funny-looking orange fish with sharp spines and ugly bulging eyes that glared at me. It wasn't much bigger than some of the bait. "Save that one for the jackpot," suggested a fisherman with an overflowing gunny sack.

Finally the torture ended. "Lines up," the captain announced on the loudspeaker. Fishermen began stowing their gear, and one of them said the magic words: "How about a little poker?"

A bunch of us followed him into the galley and crowded into a booth. An old geezer in a railroad cap produced a ratty deck of cards with Hawaiian flowers on the back; it looked as if it had seen continuous service since the Battle of Gettysburg.

"Stakes are ten and twenty, right?" I asked.

"Yep. Hey, Gert, fetch us a sack of dimes."

The galley cook produced a paper sack filled with nickels, dimes, and quarters, and dumped it on the Formica table. I stared angrily at Fresh-Air Freddy, who ignored me as he bit happily into a greasy cheeseburger.

I won the cut for deal. "You boys know how to play Omaha high-low?" They looked at me blankly. "It's a great game," I explained. "You get four cards down and five in the middle, and you must use two in your hand for high and ... "

"That's not a real game," said Engineer Bill.

I replied "How about hold'em?" I asked. More blank stares. "What do you play?"

"Real poker," a player said. "Like deuces wild." "Spit in the ocean," offered another. "Sneaky Pete." "Baseball."

I sighed. David Sklansky hadn't written a single book on these games.

I dealt baseball. Everyone anted a nickel. My first upcard was a wild three. I had to match the pot for thirty cents if I wanted to keep the card.

"What the hell," I thought, and tossed in three dimes. I kept catching threes and having to match the pot. Soon my entire buy-in was in the pot, plus five dollars more. What did I care? I had made five aces! I was going to skin these farmers!

"Five aces," I said coolly.

"No good," said Engineer Bill. "I got six kings."

"Six kings! There's no such hand!" I screamed.

"You trying to tell us how to play poker, boy?" asked Engineer Bill.

I shoved him the pot.

The next game was called Indian something-or-other, and you played it by holding your unseen hole card up against your forehead. I lost another two bucks.

The slaughter continued apace for another couple of hours. I was out fifty dollars and was glaring murderously at Fresh-Air Freddy, who was stuffing an evil-looking chili dog ...

Clamping my hand to my mouth, I dashed out to the rail. My dinner went overboard, followed by my fishing rod, tackle box, the ugly orange fish — and finally Fresh-Air Freddy.

The police understood; they ruled it justifiable homicide.

# BIG DENNY WANTS TO TALK

"Hey, MAXWELL!" the voice boomed, "I want to TALK to you!" It was Big Denny. Instinctively I looked around for an open space to maneuver in because when Big Denny is angry about something — and you never know when Big Denny will be angry about something — you don't want him backing you into a corner.

"Hi, fella," I said innocently. "I didn't write something about you that bothered you, did I?"

"Naw. It's about them other writers. They write about the same thing over and over. Vegas locals are rude. Vegas locals shouldn't snarl at tourists. Vegas locals shouldn't criticize the way tourists play poker ... "

"Well, it's hard to write something original week after week."

"What would you know about writing something original?" Big Denny sneered. "Anyways, I don't mind what they write 'cause that helps me in my new job."

"Your new job? What happened to your used car lot?"

"Aw, they shut me down on a technical violation."

"Caught you filling the transmissions with sawdust again?"

"Yeah. Anyways, I want you to write a story about me 'n' my new job. You are lookin'

> *"One last time! Are you or are you not goin' to write a article about how much friendlier us California locals are?"*

at the newly appointed Public Relations Director and Ambassador of Good Will for the California Card Casinos. My mission," he said proudly, "will be to entice and attract new patrons into the clubs."

"How, by threatening to sit on their heads?"

Big Denny's left eye began to twitch, a trick he copied from Clint Eastwood. I moved further away from a wall.

"Look," he said, grabbing my shirt, "all us regulars here in California are real ladies and gents. We treat tourists like they was rich relatives."

"How about the time a tourist check-raised you and you pushed his head into a bowl of chicken noodle soup?"

"It was matzoh ball soup," he corrected. "Wasn't even hot. But the locals here never say nothin' nasty."

"What about the time when Dirty Wally got into a beef with a Japanese guy and told the guy that during World War II he shot his old man out of a coconut tree?" I asked.

"Aw, Wally's just a colorful old coot. He's harmless."

"Tell that to the guy he shot out of the coconut tree."

"That was different. Nobody does nothin' violent here."

"How about the time you overturned a table just because you were down a hundred bucks?"

"A mistake," said Big Denny. "Actually, I was even. I figured out later I ordered a hundred dollars worth of food. Anyways, I don't do that no more. I'm a real sweet guy now."

"Then why did one of the clubs have you playing from inside a cage last night?"

"A publicity stunt," he shrugged.

"Denny, you know as much about public relations as Saddam Hussein. That movie about a guy who bites off people's faces — *The Silence of the Lambs* — hired you as technical advisor."

Big Denny was getting annoyed. "Let's not talk about me no

more. The regulars here wouldn't never do nothin' unsporting like they do in Vegas."

"No? I have yet to see Ralph the Rattler bet a lock without first complaining, 'I guess you got me'."

"OK, forget the players. There's lots of reasons to come to California instead of Vegas. They serve healthy food here, sundried tomatoes, goat cheese ... "

"Denny, the only sun-dried food you ever ate in your life was sun-dried potato chips. And you wouldn't eat goat cheese unless the entire goat came with it."

"ONE LAST TIME! Are you or are you not goin' to write a article about how much friendlier us California locals are?"

"No! Our locals are just as mean, and bloodthirsty, and rude, and sarcastic as they are in Vegas, or anywhere else for that matter. They live by the motto that good guys finish last. I have my principles and I'm not going to demean our locals by saying that California poker players are a crew of well-mannered, effete sissies."

"OK, then, let's pretend your head is an ostrich egg," Big Denny said, "and see how long it takes me to hatch it."

On reflection, I've decided that playing poker in California is a total experience unmatched anywhere else. So come to our clubs and make wonderful new friends at the table. Bask in the warm glow of players who, despite the fact that they must beat you any way they can to buy food, would never try to intimidate you or act uncivilized. And if you see some guy in a cage biting the heads off chickens, remember it's only a publicity stunt.

# TEACH ME TONIGHT

**W**hat are the most dreaded words a poker player can hear? "Collection time," you guess.

No, not that.

How about when you turn over a full house and an opponent sneers, "Get it fixed." That's bad, but still not the worst.

Well, let's say you're in a home game, you get a big check from someone you've never met before, and he asks you to "hold it for a few days." No, dear readers, the most chilling thing you can hear is someone (invariably a lady) saying, "Teach me how to play poker."

For a brief moment, you're elated that someone recognizes your expertise. Then reality — and resentment — sets in. Would someone dare approach Beethoven and ask him how to go about writing a symphony? Would someone plead with Dr. Michael DeBakey to learn how to do open-heart surgery ... in one night? Would you ask Tom Cruise how to become *Top Gun* in an F-16 fighter jet? Here you've spent years and years — a whole lifetime — learning the intricacies and subtleties of this astonishingly complex game, and some bubblehead wants to "learn it" in one lesson!

"I've got some nice books that can help you," you say sweetly, reaching for one of those eight-page booklets put out by playing-card companies and appropriately titled "Poker for Beginners," subtitled "Fourteen Interesting Home Games to Keep a Three-Year-Old Happy and Occupied."

"No you don't," she snaps. "I don't want to read some stupid book. I want(!) you(!) to(!) teach(!) me!"

"But a book is so much better organized to help you get started," I persist.

"My mind doesn't work that way. I must undergo a meaningful personal involvement to achieve enlightenment," she says, sounding just like Shirley MacLaine. "Look, you so-and-so," she adds. "You gonna teach me or not?"

I succumb to her blandishments and on the appointed night, dig out a deck and some chips and set them up on the kitchen table.

My friend arrives. "Teach me poker," she demands.

I clear my throat and begin my prepared introduction. "Poker is a contest of incomplete information in which knowledge of card and pot odds are combined with psychological thought to determine a strategy of placing bets in order to win pots either by holding the best hand or by bluffing to induce opponents with better cards to fold." I took a breath.

"What does that mean?" she asks.

I squeeze my eyes shut for a moment. This will be a long night. OK, I think. Let's break this down into A-B-C and start from the beginning. "Poker," I begin again, "is a game where everyone gets five cards. The one with the best hand wins." I began explaining the rank of each card.

"Why is a one bigger than a two?" my friend demanded, and now I knew this was going to end up being the longest night of my life.

"Those are aces and deuces," I said patiently. "An ace is the highest card in the deck because, well, just because. Actually, it is the lowest card if the game is low. Except, of course, if the low game is deuce-to-seven, in which case the ace is the *highest* card."

"Are you being smart with me?"

"No, honest," I assured my friend. "Poker is a very complicated game, especially lowball."

My friend thinks for a moment. "OK, then let's just stick to highball. What's the best hand you can get?"

"A royal flush."

"Then that's what I'll play for."

"Look, the only place they make royal flushes is in the movies. In real life, you make one every ten years."

"Then I guess you've made seven or eight so far."

"You'll notice I am ignoring your sarcasm," I said, evenly. "That is because the most important thing in poker is to keep your emotions under control and not get excited.

"Now, the odds of being dealt a royal flush are ... " I flip through a poker book ... "649,739-to-1."

"Don't confuse me with numbers and odds," she screeches. "I hate numbers and odds. I never could understand them."

"But that's what poker is all about!" I yell. "How do you expect to play poker if you don't understand the odds?"

"I'll just *feel* what's the best hand," she says, smiling sweetly. "I'm very good at that."

I rush to the bathroom to splash cold water on my face and bang my head against the wall a few times. I regain my composure and return. "I'm sorry about losing my temper," I apologize. "Keeping control isn't always easy. We will now proceed with the instruction, and I will explain the ranking of hands."

I move up the ladder from one pair to two pair, to three-of-a-kind, to a straight, to a flush.

"Is one color of flush higher than another?" she interrupts.

"That's a very good question, and the answer is no. In poker, all suits have equal ranking."

"That's stupid," she says. "In bridge, spades beat the other colors."

"This is not (expletive deleted) bridge!"

My friend inspects her fingernails. "I thought it was important to keep control of your emotions."

I go back to the bathroom and enlarge the hole in the wall. I return, still shaking slightly.

"Look," she says with some logic. "If you keep going to the bathroom to play woodpecker, we'll never get anywhere. Let's forget all that dumb talk and just play some hands."

"Fine. Anything you say," I mumble. I try to regain the upper hand by flourishing a trick riffle, and the cards spray off the table.

"Forget the fancy stuff, and let's have some money to play with," she demands.

I take out a batch of chips and give each of us a couple of piles. She looks at them suspiciously. "We professionals call these chips or checks," I explained as I dealt a sample hand and laid down some chips. "First you check your hole cards. With a good hand, you bet your checks, and with a poor hand, you check your bet."

"Check this, sucker!" she said, drawing back her fist. "And another thing. How come you have more chips than I do?"

"Look, it doesn't matter!" I yell. "This isn't real money. We're not playing a real game. I'm just showing you how it works."

"I don't care. I want the same amount of chips you have."

As mockingly as I can, I make a big production of evening up the stacks. "The yellow chips are five dollars and the blues are ten," I explain.

"Why?"

"Why what?"

"Why are the blue chips worth more than the yellow? Yellow is the stronger, ascendant primary color. It represents the power of the sun. Shirley MacLaine says ... "

"(Expletive deleted) *Shirley MacLaine!*" I scream, totally out of control. "(Expletive deleted) the yellow chips and power of the sun! Make 'em anything you want. Make 'em worth a million dollars. Make 'em ... "

"I'm sorry I got you upset," my friend said soothingly. "Now, watch your emotions and please deal out some hands. I promise not to say anything else to unnerve you."

"Give me a minute to go into the bathroom again," I requested. I enlarge the hole in the wall some more and consider what game to deal. I consider Omaha high-low but decide that would be too sadistic a punishment.

"I'll deal a game called hold'em," I announce when I return to the living room.

"What a silly name for a game. What are you supposed to hold?"

"You hold two cards," I snarl. "Or hold your two elbows. If you want, you can even hold your two ..."

"Don't you dare say that, you swine," she says quickly. "Look, if you're so emotional, why did you even ask me to learn poker from you? Maybe it would be better if you just took me to one of your card clubs and I could watch. When do you usually go?"

"Great idea," I agree. "I like to go right after the first of the month."

"Why then?"

"Because," I reply without thinking, "that's when everybody gets social security checks."

"You little rat," she spits at me. "You mean to tell me you deliberately go down there to steal pension checks from poor, sweet, old grandmothers wearing shawls?"

"Look," I defend myself. "Some of those poor, sweet, old grandmothers in shawls were playing poker before I was born, and they'd cut out your pancreas for a nickel."

"You're a beast, a horrid beast," she cries. "I never want to see you again ... until next Thursday."

"What's Thursday?"

"That's when I'm coming by for my next lesson. Is it OK if I bring my friend, Linda?"

# POTZER POKER

Not long ago I got a phone call from my older brother Ira who lives in a retirement village in New Jersey where he plays poker with a bunch of other *potzers*. I think they play nothing but seven-card stud and draw. They have never even heard of low games, much less high-tech creations like Omaha high-low split.

"Hey, baby brother," he greeted me, "I've got a question for you about poker." People are always bothering me with questions but that's the price one pays for being a poker celebrity and authority.

"What is it?" I asked. "Something to do with pot odds, positional considerations, ante structure, tells?"

"Never heard of those things," my brother said in a puzzled tone. "But there's this guy Abe in our game. Whenever I shuffle the deck and give it to him to cut, he shuffles it a few more times. What's the rule on that?"

I sighed. The old shuffle and reshuffle minuet. "No such thing as rules for home games," I said. "That would end the arguments, which are half the fun. Just tell him that his distrust is a stain on the honor of the Shapiro escutcheon."

"Oh, he trusts me," my brother assured me. "He says he has to shuffle the cards because he's nervous."

"What's he got to be nervous about? Your top bet is only a nickel."

"We just raised it to six cents."

"Oh, that's different. In that case, tell Abe to take a Valium."

"He also says I don't shuffle the cards enough."

"How many times *do* you shuffle?"

"About eighteen or twenty."

"That should do it. Look, just tell old Abe you'll allow him one riffle."

"What's a riffle?"

"A single shuffle. Two riffles make a ruffle, two ruffles make a shiffle, and two shiffles make a shuffle."

"Are you getting smart with me, baby brother?"

"No more than usual. Look, I'm a busy man. Have I answered your question?"

"No. After Abe reshuffles and cuts the cards, I shuffle and cut again just so he won't have the satisfaction. Then *he* wants to cut the deck again. Is that legal?"

"Yes. No. I don't know. Whatever makes you happy. Are we through?"

"No, there's another problem. When this player named Ed is on my right and I ask him to cut, he won't do it. He says he trusts me. Can we force him to cut?"

"No, you can't force him. Give the deck to the player on *his* right to cut."

"That would be Sid. We won't let him cut."

"Why not?" I asked with increasing despair.

"Because Sid doesn't cut just once like a normal person. He divides the deck into eight teeny-weeny little parts, and when he puts it back together, the cards are exactly the same as when he started. The man's a *schmo*."

"Tell Sid he can cut only once. Is that it?"

"No. This other player named Julie drives us crazy, because he's always calling for a cut in the middle of a hand."

"Why?"

"He says it's for luck."

"Tell Julie he's lucky you don't throw him out of the game. OK, tell him he can call for a cut whenever he wants, but each time, he'll have to add one of your nickel bets to the pot."

"Six cents."

"Excuse me, six cents. IS THAT IT?!"

"Not exactly. Herman is mad because we won't let him deal."

"Why won't you let Herman deal?"

"Because he drops cards on the floor."

"So what? I don't think you guys are playing with a full deck in the first place. Now, is that your last question about poker?"

"Yes."

"Thank God."

"But I need to ask you something about gin rummy."

"Forget it, I don't play gin. Let me give you Glenn Abney's phone number."

"Who's he?"

"He writes a gin column. He'll love to talk to you. Goodbye, Ira."

# THE NAME GAME

**W**hat's in a name? Plenty, if you're a poker player. Al the celebrated players, from the highest (Doyle "Texas Dolly" Brunson, Johnny "Oriental Express" Chan) to the lowest (Ralph the Rattler), have colorful handles. I'm sure that if I also had a memorable moniker, I'd finally get the recognition I deserve as a top-gun player. But finding an appropriate name isn't easy. Take hometown nicknames — Amarillo Slim rolls trippingly off the tongue, Oklahoma Johnny Hale sounds jaunty, and The Cincinnati Kid carries a whiff of feral danger. But somehow I don't think that Brooklyn Maxwell would make anyone wet his pants in fear.

Other legendary players, such as Puggy Pearson and Treetop Jack Straus, earned catchy names based on their appearance. Unfortunately, my most noticeable physical trait is the wide part in my hair, and I'm not particularly fond of names like "Skinhead."

Then there's Dirty Wally. What about him? Well nothing, really, but he said he'd pay me ten bucks if I mentioned him.

Anyway, I asked Sharon, a great admirer of mine, to suggest a good name. She told me to describe my key traits as a player and I, of course, selected my piercing intelligence and my total recall. "I think 'Forgetful Max' or just plain 'Dummy' would be about right," she sniffed.

I decided to seek out an authority on the subject: L.A. Jay Moriarty. L.A. Jay is a television scriptwriter who started a private tournament called *Aces and Eights* twenty years ago. Along the way, he dreamed up colorful nicknames for many of his playing buddies. The rammer-jammers earned such sobriquets as Action Al the Gambler's Pal, Zip (for zipping chips around) Vitullo, Freight-

Train Brody, Yarm the Arm, and Crazy Man Glenn Cozen). Then there are the likes of Lookie-Loo Felder, Last-Card Larry, Jimmy the Shill, and many more in Jay's bestiary. I asked Jay for a nickname that went well with "Max."

"That's a tough one," he replied hesitantly. "I know a lot of Maxes, but they're all dogs." (It really thrills me that the most popular name for a dog is now Max. Whatever happened to Spot and Rover?) Jay finally came up with Max the Ax. Not bad, but it reminded me too much of a player I know named Bernie the Butcher whose appellation gruesomely describes his meat-cleaver style of play as much as his job as a meatcutter.

Finally I asked my pal Break-Even Benny for a good name and he suggested "Rocky."

"Pretty good," I said. "Does that mean I'm a gritty, courageous fighter who gets off the canvas to win?"

"No. That means you are a rock."

Coming from Benny, that was the ultimate insult. He's called Break-Even because he always breaks even, and he always breaks even because he's never been known to play a hand. Well, two, maybe, and both times they sent camera crews. He plays at a weekly home game but only so he can eat. After polishing off a humongous dinner, he fills a bowl the size of a satellite dish with fruit salad, then munches away for hours like a cow with four stomachs. In the last game, he somehow managed to lose four stacks. That posed a greater mystery than the disappearance of Judge Crater, because, as usual, he didn't play one hand. But the puzzle was solved after he stopped off for a pastrami sandwich nightcap on the way home. He got stomach pains, and a fluoroscope exam revealed that he had swallowed four green rebuy chips. He had mistaken them for kiwi slices.

Anyway, I still haven't found any stirring nicknames. Ah, the hell with it. Call me anything. Call me ... Ishmael.

# A LEGEND IN HIS OWN MIND

**W**hen the Bicycle Club Casino in Bell Gardens California, announced plans for a *Legends of Poker Tournament,* it named such legendary players as Johnny Chan, Phil Hellmuth Jr., and Barbara Enright as hosts These were all champions who among them owned just about every title in poker. In fact,there was only one peculiar name in the whole line-up.

Mine.

As soon as the news broke, my post office box began filling with hate mail. People demanded to know if it was a typographical error, or perhaps just a sick joke. They complained that using replacement baseball players during a strike was bad enough, but that this was ridiculous. Words like "obscene" and "sacrilegious" cropped up a lot. Someone named Newt Gingrich even threatened to call for a Congressional investigation.

Obviously this is nothing but pure jealousy, and I say the heck with all of you! I earned my slot fair and square, and here's how it happened.

After I heard about the event, I went to see Robert Turner at the Bicycle Club Casino and asked if I could be one of the legends. Turner turned very pale, and then he fainted.

When he came to, he tried to call security, but could only manage a hoarse croak. Finally he regained his voice and asked why I wanted to be a tournament host.

"It's a good career move for me," I explained.

"Max," he replied kindly, "I've seen you play. A good career move for you would be to become a plumber."

Then he asked me to list the tournaments I had won.

"I haven't exactly won any tournaments," I confessed. "But once I came in sixth in a weekly twenty-dollar buy-in event."

"How many entrants were in the tournament?" Turner demanded.

"Eight. It was right after the earthquake, and the club was rather empty. And one guy had to rush home when he heard his house had collapsed, so he got blinded off," I added helpfully.

Turner was not exactly impressed, but I kept whining and wheedling until he promised to see what he could do. A few days later he phoned to say management had agreed to hire me — but only if I also performed some additional chores.

"Like what?" I asked suspiciously.

"Oh, little things, like take messages, help set up the tables, do some clean-up afterwards, relieve the guy in the hot dog stand on his breaks ..."

I agreed to everything — except for wearing fishnet stockings and serving cocktails. I think they were just testing me on that one, though.

Then I asked which tournament I could host and play in, and Turner suggested the ladies seven-stud event.

"Give me a break, Robert," I pleaded.

Then he offered me the draw tournament, but I was too sharp for him. I knew that draw wasn't even scheduled. Finally he agreed to let me host one of the Omaha high-low events, saying that even I couldn't damage a game like that. I was ecstatic. What a fine gentleman!

Two days later, my phone rang again. It was Turner, and this time I could hear angry voices in the background.

"The deal's off, Max," he told me. "The other hosts threaten to quit if I let you in."

"Suck eggs, Turner!" I yelled. "I've got a contract."

"How about if we pay you off?"

"Forget it. I can't disappoint my fans."

He asked me to hold on while he talked to the other hosts again. I could hear him pleading my case, but the shouting only grew louder and uglier. Things were being thrown. I distinctly heard one player calling for a rope.

Finally, the hubbub died down a little, and Turner picked up the phone again.

"OK, Max, I've worked out a deal," he said with great weariness. "The others have agreed to let you host and play, but only on one condition."

"Name it," I said triumphantly.

"Do you mind wearing a bag over your head?"

# THE RETURN OF BIG DENNY

I was standing in the buffet line at a card club when someone nudged me from behind. Turning around, I gazed up at the formidable figure of Big Denny.

"How ya' been, Maxey?" he greeted me. "Hope you'll excuse me if I don't shake hands."

Considering that Big Denny held a turkey leg in one hand and a pork chop in the other, to say nothing of the half-chewed ham sandwich in his mouth, I did not mind forgoing that social amenity.

"C'mon over to my table and talk," he said, pointing a pork chop in the appropriate direction. We walked over, and he graciously cleared a place for me by shoving aside about a dozen of his emptied plates and wiping up part of a gravy puddle he had dribbled on the seat.

I wondered why he was being so nice. I found out when he began pitching me to play in his home game.

"No thanks," I demurred. "Last time I played at your place you raked out at least $900."

"Hey, it's expensive puttin' on a game," he protested. "Remember I ordered in forty sandwiches?"

"Sure, and you ate thirty-five of them yourself."

Big Denny made a threatening move toward me, and I quickly edged away — right into the remaining gravy. Well, better gravy stains than blood stains, I figured. "Another thing," I added. "Joe Hawkins told me that at your last game you got stuck, so you locked the doors and wouldn't let anybody out until you got even."

Denny shrugged. "No big deal. The game just ran a little longer than usual."

"Four days?"

"Forget it," Big Denny spat in disgust. "Who needs you anyways; you're tighter than Roseanne Arnold's girdle."

Suddenly, another thought crossed his mind. "Say, when did they stop servin' lox at this place?" he demanded crossly.

"When they saw you coming," I told him. "You're not supposed to put the whole salmon on your plate. They claim you drove up the price of lox to twenty dollars a pound single-handedly by wiping out this season's entire salmon run."

Big Denny waved his hand, spattering me with gravy from the pork chop he still held in his fist. "Never mind about that. I got a bone I want to pick with you."

I looked around at the rubble he had left on the table. "Looks like you've picked about a hundred bones already."

Denny made another move toward me. I slid over further, this time into some mashed potatoes he had dropped. "You've been writin' some real junk in your columns lately," he smirked. "How come you never write about me no more?"

"For one thing," I reminded him, "you threatened to kill me if I did."

"Aw, don't be so sensitive," he said. "I only got sore that time when you said I mal... mal... "

"Maliciously?"

"Yeah, maliciously broke some guy's fingers when I worked here as a security guard."

"Well, didn't you?"

Big Denny flung his arms apart to show his innocence, spraying me with bits of pork chop from one hand and some of the chili dog from his other hand. "Nothin' malicious about it. The bum was tryin' to sneak an extra pack of Sweet 'n' Low from the restaurant."

"Oh, I didn't know that. How's the lawsuit going?"

"We settled outta court. He agreed to drop the case if I agreed not to sit on his head."

"Denny," I said, "why don't you stick to things you know, like selling lemons to suckers at your car lot?"

"They shut me down again," he grumbled.

"What was it this time — turning back the odometer? Putting sawdust in the transmissions?"

"Naw, some jerk complained 'cause he found a body in the trunk of a car I sold him."

"You're getting careless, Denny."

"Yeah, that's the last time I take a trade-in from a guy named Vinny."

"So what will you do until they lift your suspension?"

"Well, I had this great idea and I wanted your opinion."

"What's the great idea?"

"Whadda ya think about me openin' a charm school?"

# HUSTLERS AND HAYSEEDS: HOW TO DIFFERENTIATE

I hate it when some wise guy sits down at the table and goes into a stupid routine that's supposed to make you think he's never played before: "What's this game called? Hold'em? Do you have to use both cards?"

Sure. There he is with clear fingernail polish and headphones, rolling chips up one arm and down the other, and we're supposed to think he came to town on the 5:15 turnip truck.

That's the trouble with poker — honest amateur sportsmen like me have to compete with professional wolves who baa like sheep. In no other sport are these pro-amateur mismatches allowed. Nolan Ryan can't pitch Little League, for example. But, a *World Series of Poker* champion could tear up your nice little $3-$6 game if he had a mind to.

Why should these pros be allowed to play on equal terms with us purists? Heavyweights don't box welterweights. Formula 1 drivers don't race go-karts. Amateur golfers get handicaps. Fast racehorses carry lead in their saddles.

I say even things up the same way in poker. Make pros play with an exposed card; deal the amateurs an extra card. In tournaments give the pros fewer chips for their buy-ins. Or, put lead in *their* saddles.

The problem is, it's hard to spot professionals. Most of them seem like normal, respectable people. I say, force them to carry ID markings, like prisoners on work detail with a big letter "P" emblazoned on their backs. Make the money players wear the same "P" for "pro," I say. Only on their heads. And make the letter scarlet. Sew hash marks on their sleeves to designate years of experience, the way they do in the Army.

Even if you recognize a pro, how do you know how good he is? They all lie. Poker players aren't ranked like tennis players or Grand Prix race drivers. How about campaign ribbons to show what tournaments they've won?

Now, some pros *do* carry identifying symbols. Johnny Chan, for example, plays with an orange on the table. How about the others? Make Johnny Moss play with a prune, for example.

All right, all right. I know I'm getting silly. Ringers don't carry neon signs. So let me offer some subtle clues to help you separate the hustlers from the hayseeds.

To start, hayseeds have normal color in their cheeks from working in daylight at honest jobs. Hustlers are as pallid as Dracula because that's how seldom they see the sun.

Hayseeds overtip. They're so overjoyed and incredulous when they win a hand that they tip everyone in sight. If the Wicked Witch of the West walked by, they'd tip her. When a hustler feels compelled to tip, it's strictly minimum wage, with a pained look on his face, except for off-duty dealers. They're the most lavish tippers in the world. Of course, with them, it's not really tipping. They're practicing behavior modification on the other players.

When a hustler bets, he'll drop down a row of chips like a B-52 that's carpet-bombing a battlefield. Pow! Pow! Pow! When a hayseed bets, he'll fumble out one chip at a time in a messy jumble, lose count halfway through, and start over.

When a hayseed wants to check, he'll wave his arms around and ask, "Who's it on? Me? Oh. What's the bet? Nobody bet? Oh, I pass, I mean, check." When a hustler checks, he silently raises his forefinger a quarter inch off the table. Hustlers do not care to waste energy.

When a hustler raises. he'll quietly slide in his chips. When a hayseed raises, he'll make some inane home-game comment like, "Up the slope goes the antelope."

Hustlers speak the language of poker. "I had seventeen outs and missed," one might grumble. A hayseed will ask, "What's an out?" To a hayseed, a double belly-buster is a woman pregnant with twins.

Hustlers rarely look at their hole cards more than once. Hayseeds have to examine them each round, in case the cards change, I suppose.

Win or lose, hayseeds are always grinning like idiots. A hustler may have chips piled to the ceiling, but he's always scowling. He never thinks he's winning as much as he should.

Finally, hayseeds are embarrassed by their ineptitude. They're always apologizing for taking too long, for betting out of turn, for putting in the wrong amount of chips. If a hayseed had a heart attack, he'd apologize for slowing down the game. A hustler wouldn't apologize if he dumped hot coffee in your lap. He'd expect you to buy him a refill.

# SECTION THREE

# Where the Winners Tell Jokes ...

I cannot forecast to you the action of Russia. It is a riddle
wrapped in a mystery inside an enigma.
*Sir Winston Churchill*

(The same can be said for the action of Omaha high-low.)
*Max Shapiro*

# BAD-BEAT HEALTH CARE

**B**ill Clinton goofed. He spent a whole year working out a comprehensive health care package and then left out the most important element of all: a provision for bad-beat therapy.

I mean, it's fine to be covered for things like a bleeding gizzard, but what a poker player really wants and needs is a good listener to bitch to when some fool snaps off his lock hand with a miracle catch.

As things stand now, who you gonna call, Ghostbusters? 911? Oprah? A lot of good it does to complain to another player. He doesn't give a rat's ass about your problems; he'll either yawn in your face or, worse, bore you with his *own* bad-beat stories.

I'm not being silly here. It is absolutely critical to a poker player's mental health to be able to avail himself of a trained and sympathetic ear in bad-beat emergencies.

But I'm not sure if government control is the answer. You'd have to wait weeks for an appointment to a bad-beat medical clinic, only to be handed over to some croaker who'd give everyone the same canned, insincere response: "That's the worst beat I ever heard. You sure were unlucky. Next."

This really is a worldwide problem, you know. For example, I have an Israeli friend who plays a lot of poker in his native country. Every time he gets outdrawn he runs out to the "Wailing Wall" in Jerusalem and complains for hours to God.

"Does God ever answer you?" I once asked.

"Are you kidding?" he said. "It's like talking to a wall."

But this gave me what I thought was a great idea: installing confessional booths at the card clubs. I'd charge five dollars for the first three minutes, plus another dollar for a jackpot drop.

"I have sinned, father. I gave this sucker a free card and he filled an inside straight."

But then I learned my scheme was illegal. It violated the separation of church and straights.

For a while I considered those medical emergency devices that dotty old ladies wear around their necks in television commercials. You'd press a button to trigger an alarm in a bad-beat monitoring station, and they'd send out a paramedic to listen to you. But with a bad-beat victim's luck, the battery probably would go dead just when you needed it.

I kept working on the problem, and eventually came up with the answer: a bad-beat telephone hotline!

Look, today you can get almost anything by phone ... ball scores, stock quotes, weather reports, dentist referrals, dial-a-prayer, dial-a-joke, whatever. If you need to know the future, you can call a psychic hotline. If you're "lonely," you can dial up phone sex. So why not a customized bad-beat counseling service?

Here's how it will work. First you dial 976-BAD-BEAT. Then a soothing voice will say, "You have reached the Bad-Beat Hotline. If you want technical reinforcement, please press one. If you would like to speak to a sympathetic, Jewish mother, press two ..."

Here are some of the typical responses you can expect:

*Technical Reinforcement:* A no-nonsense Mason Malmuth type will reassure you, "A back-door flush? He was a 23-to-1 underdog. You played correctly and enjoy a positive expectation for future situations."

*Jewish Mother:* "That's terrible what he did to you. Don't worry, he'll be punished, that *gonif.* Eat a nice hot bowl of chicken soup, you'll feel better. And call your mother often. It's only two dollars a minute."

*Freudian Psychiatrist:* "I see. Tell me what you are feeling now. You want to know what to do? What do *you* think you should do?"

*Masochistic Abuse:* "You loser! You *schlemiel!* You're just a hard-luck good-for-nothing who doesn't know the first thing about playing poker!"

You see the possibilities? And just think of what this will do to jump-start the economy. You could take all those busted-out players off the rail and put them to work manning the phones. Instead of having to listen to their woes, you make them listen to yours.

Best of all, each caller would be eligible for the annual bad-beat championship playoffs. I tell you, it would be bigger than the *Pillsbury Bakeoff.*

Finalists would be judged in two categories: technical and artistic. Technical points would be awarded for such criteria as size of the pot, ineptitude of your opponent, and odds against the beat. Bonus points will be awarded if the beat busted you or knocked you out of a tournament.

Artistic judging will measure the quality and drama of your presentation and the copiousness of your tears. Bonus points will be awarded for such little touches as beating your breast, rending your garments, and setting yourself on fire.

The winning loser will receive a year's supply of sackcloth and ashes and an all-expense-paid trip to the Dunes Hotel in Las Vegas.

# CASINO CALISTHENICS

Rated for its health benefits, poker as a sport would fall somewhere between alligator wrestling and Russian roulette. Sitting motionless for hours, wolfing down greaseburgers, absorbing heart-stopping bad beats, and blackening one's lungs with secondhand cigarette smoke is not exactly the prescription for a long and vigorous life.

Face it, when is the last time you saw a poker player on Willard Scott's hundred-year-old birthday greeting list?

But after studying this problem for a long time, I've designed some simple isometric and aerobic exercises which can be performed unobtrusively at the table.

Here then, for the first time anywhere, is the complete guide to casino calisthenics.

*The Table-Lift Chip Dump:* You're at a table where someone on a rush has accumulated a mass of chips. Rather than stack the chips the way a normal person would, this clown aggravates everyone by gleefully constructing two towering turrets. What you must do is brace your upper legs under the table, lift it as high as you can, and then suddenly *drop it!* This exercise will greatly strengthen your quadriceps (front thigh muscles) and, if performed correctly, will also knock down the clown's chip towers.

*The Three-Lap Casino Run:* This splendid aerobic exercise will follow when the clown discovers you were the culprit and chases you around the cardroom floor — a fine routine for building lung capacity.

*The Neck-Stretching Hole-Card Peek:* To perform this exercise, act as if you are limbering up your sore neck muscles. Rotate your head a couple of times, then stretch your neck first w-a-a-y to the right, then w-a-a-y to the left. This will accomplish three things. You will indeed ease any neck stiffness, you will build up the sternocleidomastoids muscles in your neck, and, if timed correctly, you will glimpse your opponents' hole cards.

*The Jackpot Hour Thigh-Clamp:* Your bladder is bursting, but there's fifteen minutes of triple-jackpot time left, and you dare not miss a hand. Squeeze your thighs together as tightly as you can. *Hold in this position.* This contraction exercise will develop the adductor magnus, which is the largest of the five muscles composing the medial or inner thigh. Deep groaning may also help.

*The 100-Yard Restroom Dash:* Alternately, you may wish to attempt a quick sprint up and back in time so you do not miss a hand. You can even make this a competitive sport by timing yourself. Award yourself extra points for stopping to wash your hands, and for every old lady you knock down along the way.

*The Bad-Beat Silent Scream:* This is both a physical and psychological exercise to be performed immediately after an especially bad, bad beat. Tense the muscles around your mouth and jaw into a death rictus, and silently, from within, emit the most agonizingly anguished cry you can muster. This is a superb exercise for firming your facial muscles and is a preferable alternative to jabbing a fork into your chest.

*The Server-Summons Spring:* The most basic calisthenic, familiar to anyone who was in the Army, is the "jumping jack."

It is performed by jumping up and down while swinging your arms high overhead and clapping your hands together. This is an excellent exercise, but if you try it at the table, the security guards are likely to drop a net over your head. Here's the trick: While doing jumping jacks, yell "Service!" at the top of your lungs. That way you'll seem no different from hundreds of other players in the cardroom, futilely trying to summon a food server. (Did you ever notice that it takes two hours on average to get a food server to come over, and less than ten minutes before a porter swipes your cart away when you're only half-finished eating?)

*The Windshield Wiper Maneuver:* If another player's cigarette smoke is drifting past your nose, rhythmically wave your hand back and forth like a wiper blade in a rainstorm. The longer and more vigorously you perform this exercise, the more you will strengthen your wrist muscles, and the more likely that you will infuriate the smoker and put him on tilt.

# TIPPING

Tipping is both an art and a science, and I'm about to explain everything you'll ever need to know about this misunderstood practice.

To begin, don't tip emotionally. How often have you raked in a gigantic pot and euphorically flung a triple toke to the splendid fellow who made you rich? His "Thank you, sir!" falls pleasantly on your ears and you feel like a prince on horseback tossing coins to the peasants. Other times, you're deep in the hole, win a modest pot, and resent tipping the lout who dug that hole for you in the first place.

Wrong, wrong, wrong, all wrong. Tipping isn't personal. You treat it as a business. For example, many players think dealers can affect the outcome of hands. "Tip" supposedly stands for "to insure promptness," but some folks think it stands for "to insure pots." So they dispense chips as a form of sacrifice to appease the dealer-god and stay in his good graces.

But if that's true, why bother tipping after you've won?

The money is yours, who needs a partner then? The trick is to tip him before he deals to put him on the payroll.

On the other hand, some cynics question the value of tipping — ever. "Dealers don't do nuttin' for me," they grouse. Untrue. Say you've been feebly yelping for service for half an hour. The dealer will just smirk at non-tippers. For a big tipper, he'll bellow, "SERVICE, TABLE THIRTY-FOUR!" so loud that three food servers, two porters, a cocktail waitress and a valet parking attendant will materialize in ten seconds flat.

If you're a nontipper who smokes, the dealer will wave his hand and cough whenever you fire up. If you're a big tipper, he'll light your butt and hold the ashtray for you.

Or let's say you feel crowded and ask the dealer to space out the chairs. Nontipper? He'll suggest you go on a diet. Big tipper? He'll have the other players sit in each others laps, if that's what it takes to make you comfortable.

Knowing how much to tip isn't always easy. But there are clues to follow. For example, if the dealer throws your chip back at you, he's subtly suggesting your tip is too small. Ditto if he stares at your toke and then drops it into his tray like a dead bug. Or worse, down the collection slot.

Here are more clues. The dealer grins when you lose a pot and changes the deck when you win. He continually deals you out "by mistake." He has you picked up if you're away from the table for more than forty-five seconds.

On the other hand, you can also guard against wasteful over-tipping by watching for delicate clues in a dealer's body language. Shaking your hand, kissing you, or licking your face are all sure signs that your toking is excessive. So is letting you peek at the next card off the deck.

If the dealer says "thank you" two or three times, that's another indication. However, be careful here. If he thanks you more than three times, it may be sarcasm.

I've never been satisfied with the standard practice of handing over a standard tip for a standard pot, commonly a dollar in California and fifty cents in Las Vegas (and would someone please explain to me how this geographical disparity arose?). It's not flexible enough to cover differing situations. So I've decided to revise the etiquette of tipping by publishing my personal guidelines.

If a new dealer sits down and greets the table with a hearty, "How's everybody today?" I subtract five points. If I'm losing, I subtract another point for *every* hundred I'm down.

If the dealer keeps the game moving along by prompting slow or unconscious players, I add five points. If he rushes me, I subtract ten points.

If the dealer is a man in need of a shave, I subtract five points. If the dealer is a woman in need of a shave, I subtract ten points.

In an Omaha high-low game with four side pots, if the dealer can divide the chips correctly in under a minute, I award twenty points (and a round of applause).

I don't care for dealers who solicit tips. I subtract five points if he uses props like a picture of his wife and twelve children, or a collection can labeled "Feed the Kitty."

At the end of his shift, I figure up all the points, add one percent of the money that I've won during his shift or subtract five percent if I've lost, double it if he mentions my writing, and multiply the total by that day's Dow-Jones industrial average. The frustrating thing is that by the time I'm done figuring, the dealer usually has left the table.

But it does cut down on my tipping expense.

# SHOW THEM WHO'S BOSS

This lesson deals with the subject of domination. No, you sillies, I'm not talking about whips and chains and spankings. I mean table domination, the art of making yourself the most intimidating, commanding, and feared presence at the table; the top dog, the high kahuna, the big enchilada who subjugates and controls the other players the way the sun controls the orbits of all the planets in the solar system.

Animal behaviorists tell us that this struggle for hierarchical leadership is a natural instinct common to all creatures from sled dogs to wheel horses. Animals seek such ascendancy in various ways. Chickens do it by pecking lesser chickens (hence the term pecking order). Gorillas do it by beating their breasts and bellowing ferociously like Big Denny. Elks butt heads (especially after they've had a few beers at the local Elks Lodge). And wolves become pack leaders by chewing off the legs of challengers.

These methods are not recommended at a casino as they may get you barred. So let me suggest some other things you can do to make yourself the head honcho at your table.

*Height:* You must literally seize the high ground to look down on your subjects. This was shown in a 1940 film called *The Great Dictator* in which Charlie Chaplin played Hitler and Jack Oakie was Mussolini. In a barber shop scene, each tried to gain ascendancy over the other by ratcheting up his barber chair to ever-greater heights. You can do the same thing in a card club by stacking cushions on your seat as high as necessary. Above twelve feet, though, crash helmets and parachutes are recommended.

*Chip overkill:* My rule of thumb is to buy in for ten times as many chips as any other player at the table. And don't just stack your chips in simple columns. Employ them to construct intimidating fortresses: castles with crenellated turrets, soaring battlements, moats, drawbridges, and little containers of boiling oil perched on the highest escarpments.

*Clothing:* Remember what Shakespeare said: "Clothes make the man." (Actually, he wrote, "Apparel oft proclaims the man," but nobody uses the word "oft" much any more.) If you want your opponents to respect and be awed by you, don't wear a T-shirt with pictures of teddy bears, or one that says, "My grandma went to Disneyland, and all she bought me was this lousy T-shirt."

Dress like a substantial, successful man of means, even if you have to borrow money to do so. Wear a well-cut power suit (make sure that the jacket and pants match and are not made of polyester), a nice tie without soup stains, and impressive accessories such as a gold Rolex. It's true that a genuine gold Rolex costs up to $10,000 and may get you killed in the parking lot, but you can find a good imitation on Hollywood Boulevard for around thirty bucks. There's only one subtle way to tell the difference: the fake gold Rolex turns your arm green.

*Sunglasses:* The *ne plus ultra* of intimidating gear is a pair of dark, wraparound indoor shades. You may have trouble reading the cards, but you'll look as menacing as Arnold Schwarzenegger playing a cyborg terminator.

*Have an entourage:* Nothing will impress players more than seeing a crew of lackeys dancing attendance on you. At the minimum, have at the table a masseur, a manicurist, a shoeshine person, and a bodyguard named Gino standing around with his hand inside his jacket, calling you "Boss," lighting your cigars, and writing down the names of anyone foolish enough to beat you out of a pot. It's also important to have a good "sweater" like Dirty Wally behind you. Wally's standard fee for sweating is twenty-five dollars an hour, but on a slow day he'll settle for a hamburger. Throw in some cheese and he'll also give you a haircut.

*Talk to no one:* Do not allow any player to talk to you as if he or she were your equal. Should a player (or dealer) be rash enough to address you directly, turn to Gino and ask, "What did he say?" Let Gino tell you, "He says it's your blind, Boss."

*Announce yourself:* Finally, have yourself paged every fifteen minutes, like a starlet poolside at the Beverly Hills Hotel. But don't use your real name, especially if it's one like Myron Mertz. You need a name that deserves respect.

How about, "Don Vito Corleone."

# POKER, SPORTS, AND SPONSORS

While poker tournaments keep growing in number and popularity, compared to other sporting events they're still pretty small potatoes, and probably rank somewhere between Parcheesi and arm wrestling in national recognition. It's been pointed out that outside sponsorship could help propel tournaments into the big time and gain more exposure for them. Exposure never hurt anyone ... with the notable exception of Pee-Wee Herman, that is.

Corporations today are positively panting to put their names on just about any sporting event, no matter how dinky or bizarre. Turn on your television some Sunday afternoon. One channel might be carrying the *Pyramid Scheme Investments Golf Classic* in Fort Mudge, Arkansas, while a second is offering the *Emphysema Cigarettes Tennis Invitational,* and a third is broadcasting the *Schatzenheuser Beer Car-Crushing Trials* — though why people would pay to watch something they can see for nothing on the Hollywood Freeway is beyond me.

The list goes on and on, with every sport from beach volleyball to motocross being sponsored, and every athlete in each sport plastered from head to toe with advertising logos. The only reason nobody sponsors the *Miss Nude America Pageant* is because they can't figure out where to sew on a brand logo.

With all the hype and hoopla, these events pull thousands of fans into the stands, while millions more watch on television. By contrast, a poker tournament might squeeze in a few dozen onlookers — many of them contestants who busted out of the tourney earlier. Tournament poker is the only sport where the players outnumber the spectators, and where the players pay and the fans get in free.

All this will change once we figure out a way to attract a few deep-pocket sponsors.

Now, I'm a realist. I know some people still think poker is as immoral as bear baiting. Marketing directors fuss over their company's image, and I don't expect we'll ever see the Ovaltine Omaha High-Low Poker Classic. Still, there are many other appropriate sponsors waiting to be tapped.

Tobacco and alcoholic beverage companies, of course, are first on the list. But also, how about aspirin and antacid manufacturers, pawnbrokers, marriage counselors, therapists to listen to bad-beat stories, etc., etc.?

Of course, there's another stumbling block to attracting sponsors and TV to poker tournaments. Playing in them might be exciting, but watching them can be as thrilling as watching paint dry. Poker athletes don't get whacked on the head with sticks as in hockey; there are no fiery crashes as in auto racing — just a bunch of guys sitting around a table glaring at one another and pushing chips back and forth.

Another depressing aspect is that most poker players dress as if they're taking out the garbage — and some of them look like their clothes *came* from the garbage. A Pennzoil patch that looks zippy on Mario Andretti's racing suit would be somewhat less dashing on Seymour Leibowitz's suspenders.

No way around it: poker tournaments need more pizzazz and show business. And the shining example to emulate is that incredible melange of contrived junk sport called American Gladiators. This "sport" features a bunch of studs and studesses in green and orange leotards climbing walls, swinging from ropes, rolling around in barrels, and bashing each other with padded clubs. All it lacks are lions to eat the losers.

If that's what it takes, let's do the same for poker.

Let's dress tournament players in iridescent jumpsuits, glow-in-the-dark cowboy hats, and similar finery. When a player busts out, instead of offering a polite round of applause, beat him on the noggin with those padded sticks. Bring in dance hall cheerleaders to perform during the tournament breaks. Add gimmicks to make the game more exciting. For example, from time to time have a duck drop down from the ceiling — like on the old Groucho Marx game show — and when that happens all the deuces are wild.

Bring in a Howard Cosell-type for the play-by-play: "We are witnessing the denouement of a grueling confrontation, ladies and gentlemen, where an embattled combatant stares unflinchingly into the gaping jaws of defeat and draws on a Herculean reserve of indomitable courage ..."

Remember, our most popular games didn't take off until some innovation caught the fancy of fans: the forward pass in football, the three-pointer in basketball, the eye-gouge in wrestling. With similar imagination, tournament poker can some day take its deserved place in the front rank of sport.

# SCIENTIFIC RECORD KEEPING AND OTHER LUCKY MOVES

P oker writers constantly exhort us serious players to keep records. I'm in favor of that. It's just that I have a different idea of what records are important to keep.

We're told to keep track of such mundane things as what clubs we were at, hours played, stakes, type of game, caliber of opponents, and similar nonsense. I even read something about recording standard deviation. How do you do that? It's true that most of the players I know are deviants, but I wouldn't call any of them standard.

Forget all that junk and take note of those things I have found to be really important to chart.

One of the most significant factors is what you wear during a game. If you won, that means you were wearing something lucky and you must keep wearing the same things to keep your streak going, or conversely, change should you lose. In my case, this has had a salubrious effect on my personal hygiene. Since I win so seldom, I am compelled to rotate my underwear constantly. Luckily, I do own two pairs of shorts.

Almost as important is the direction you are facing when seated at the table. I am convinced that magnetism affects our thought processes and our luck, and it is vital to be properly aligned. Don't scoff; magnetism is a force to be reckoned with. It's what birds use to find their way around ... or did you think they used a gas station map?

Keep meticulous records of what food you order at the club. If you find that you've won three times in a row after you ate moo goo gai pan, but lost three consecutive sessions after dining on fried okra, obviously something in the moo goo gai pan is making your brain work better or bringing you more luck than the okra. To narrow it down even further, try ordering just the moo or just the goo a few times to determine which element in the food is doing the trick.

The next thing is so obvious it hardly needs repeating, but be sure to keep tabs on which dealers you win and lose with. Some of them regularly beat you like an ugly stepchild and some turn all your hands into gold like King Midas. I'm not certain why this happens, but I suspect it has something to do with your astrological signs. So it might be a good idea to get the dealers' birth signs and have your respective charts worked up. If a dealer comes to your table when her moons are descending into your third house of Saturn, you'd be well advised to take a dinner break and eat some moo goo gai pan.

It's also helpful to know the year in which the dealers were born. In the Chinese Zodiac, each of the twelve years is ruled by a different animal. Different animals get along splendidly while others are natural-born enemies. So if you're under the sign of the horse, for example, you should do well with a dog dealer but expect to be bitten by a rat dealer.

I see some of you out there are complaining that this is getting too complicated. Well, nobody said poker was an easy game to master. And isn't this why you read books ... to get valuable advice? So quit whining and read on.

Take careful note in your records of the day of the month. No, this has nothing to do with astrological signs, but something even more important. You want to be aware of when the old folks get their social security checks.

Now, some players are superstitious enough to think that all they need to win is any old lucky charm. I never cease to be amazed at the ignorance that still abounds in this supposedly enlightened age. Don't they realize that the luck that's in a charm wears down and must be replenished? After all, even the Energizer Bunny has to replace his batteries from time to time. So if your records indicate that the magic in your rabbit's foot is starting to ebb, give it a rest and bring in a fresh charm like a teddy bear or a shrunken head.

I have found these records nearly infallible in charting my success ratio. Of course, sometimes they do need a minor fine-tuning. For example, I see that on November 7, I wore my lucky underwear, faced directly into the magnetic stream, ate the moo goo gai pan with extra moo, brought a fresh teddy bear, faced a succession of dog-sign dealers with ascending moons, and still lost eighty-eight dollars in a $1-$2 Omaha game.

Maybe I had an unlucky cocktail server. Maybe if I worked up horoscopes on all the floormen and added that data to my records ...

# CASTING THE ROLE OF A CHAMP

I t's been suggested that there might be a better way to select the poker champion of the world than by a single no-limit Texas hold'em tournament. David Sklansky, for example, has recommended an "octagonal" structure using eight different games with one played every thirty minutes. And Glenn Cozen, runner-up in the 1993 *World Series of Poker* championship event, likes a dealer's choice format.

I also favor a multiple-game approach but I'd go even further in order to bring the championship into the 90s. Since my ideas are so respected and influential in poker circles, I have been asked to outline them here.

First, I would weight each game according to the level of skill needed. On this basis I would award Omaha high-low seventy-five percent of the points. I would also introduce into the mix five-card Omaha and reverse Omaha (you play three cards from your hand and two from the board). The remaining games don't matter much — hold'em, I suppose, and whatever else there is. I myself don't know any other games.

But the tournament itself would be only part of the selection process, for it should take more than just card sense and luck for a man (or woman) to become a fully realized champion.

Let me use the Miss America competition as an illustration. Once upon a time, a contestant needed only to look good in a bathing suit. If she had great legs, a blinding smile, and was brainy enough to walk down a runway without falling off the stage, she got crowned.

No more. This is the age of the liberated woman, with talent counting as much as sex appeal. So we are now forced to watch these beauty contestants play the accordion, sing off key, and make nauseating little speeches. Today they want a complete Miss America with looks, personality, and the ability to recite poetry.

The same criteria should apply to the reigning poker champ. The thing to remember is that this top dog player is the symbol and spokesperson for our game for the next twelve months. He should look and sound like a top dog gambler, by gum, the way the general public and the media expect him to.

You know, like James Garner or Mel Gibson as *Maverick,* or Tyrone Power as the *Mississippi Gambler,* or Steve McQueen as the *Cincinnati Kid.* The public and the press don't care about someone who resembles an accountant or a gas company repairman. And if someone who looks like me ever won the *World Series,* that would probably finish it.

Meaning no disrespect, but too many of the more recent winners have looked, well, ordinary. They just lack the presence of a Doyle Brunson or a Puggy Pearson. I mean, you would have a hard time picking them out of a police line-up.

Even their names often lack marquee appeal. Why, we once had someone named Bill Smith take down the title. Sure, he's one hell of a poker player, but does the name "Bill Smith" grab you like "Doc Holliday" does?

Now, the one champ who epitomizes the way a gambler is supposed to look and sound is Amarillo Slim Preston. Tall, slender as a toothpick, dressed to the nines from his Texas Stetson to his snakeskin boots, and blessed with a wonderful gift of gab, he probably got more TV exposure and publicity for the game than all the other champs combined.

So here's what I suggest. Like figure skating, award points for the poker tournament (technique) and the impression made by the player (artistry). Find someone who can walk the walk and talk the talk.

Have an artistry competition in which finalists from the last table parade around a stage in their best gamblin' gear.

Points will be awarded for the flashiest clothes, the biggest belt buckles, and the heaviest gold jewelry. Points would be deducted for suspenders and windbreakers. (Sorry, Seymour.)

Then have the contestants spin their best poker yarns.

Points will be awarded for such things as the biggest lies and the best cowboy twang or southern dialect. Points will be deducted from anyone failin' to drop their final g's.

Using these criteria, I guarantee we'll come up not only with the best player, but the best lookin', best talkin' poker fella around these here parts.

I mean, if we could cast an actor like Ronald Reagan to play the president, why can't we do the same for poker?

# WHO'S ON TILT?

I f staying off tilt is the bet thing you can do for yourself at poker, then putting someone else on tilt is the second best. While it's nice to win someone's money, if you can mess up his head at the same time, so much the better. The dictionary defines this as psychological warfare. I prefer "dirty tricks."

"Hold it!" I can hear you scream. "Poker is supposed to be an ethical game played by gentlemen — like chess."

Sure. When Rue, the legendary 16th Century Spanish chess player wrote a textbook, he advised his students always to try to place the board so that the sun or lamp would shine in the opponents' eyes.

Anything you can do in poker to distract, annoy, break the concentration, or infuriate an opponent should be considered. I didn't say you should do it; just consider it. There's nothing unethical in that, is there?

Just as it's important to watch for playing tells, you also should observe opponents for psychological tells. Notice what sort of sounds, gestures, phrases, or actions cause them to wince, frown, grimace, narrow their eyes, or turn red. Find out about their personal lives, their problems, weaknesses, and areas that can be exploited.

Timing is exquisitely important. When they're winning, happy, and confident, you begin wafting little barbs their way to unnerve them. When they're beginning to lose it, you turn up the heat. And when they're utterly demoralized and bleeding chips, you finish them off with a hard "kick."

In the novel *Hawaii,* the young hero is advised by a sea captain that when he's in a fight and has beaten an opponent, he should kick him in the face. Otherwise, he is told, in time, the victim will think you were lucky and come at you again. If you can scare him he'll always remember and fear you. Good advice.

So where to start.

To begin with, notice what sounds annoy a player. Try whistling humming, drumming your fingers. Slurp your drinks. Chew food with disgusting smacking sounds. Belch. Make post-nasal drip sniffling noises. Feign a persistent dry cough in his direction.

If he's a smoker and you're not, fan the air and cough every time he lights up. If you smoke and he doesn't, position your ashtray and exhale so he gets a maximum dose of fumes.

If you're in a private home and he complains that it's warm you insist it's too cold. And vice versa. Try surreptitiously opening windows if the draft bothers him. Close them if he says it's too stuffy.

Personal slurs are always good. Use phrases like, "The bet's on you, baldy." Or, fatso, hairlip, whatever's appropriate. If he's wearing an offbeat shirt, make fun of it. If he's heavily in the stock market and the Dow Jones has gone down that day, say "You must have taken a real beating today."

If an opponent is winning, do everything you can to turn the tide. Constantly accuse him of playing too tight or sitting on his chips. Subtly suggest he may be cheating. If he's sitting next to you, tell him to stop looking at your cards. Frequently accuse him of being light in the pot, not putting in his ante, making the wrong change.

If you get up from the table for a quick break, glance suspiciously at someone sitting next to you and take your chips with you.

If you're playing high-low split declare games, you can kill two opponents with one stone by asking how come they never seem to declare against one another.

When you're dealing, one of the best ways to unnerve a player is to expose one of his cards "accidentally."

When nothing else seems to be working, an extreme move is to knock a cup of hot coffee into his lap. Very effective, but not for the fainthearted.

Of course the very best way to switch someone into the tilt mode is to hand him a bad beat. If you're fortunate enough to have this happen, do everything you can to magnify and exploit your opportunity.

Slow-roll your victim. Let him think he's won and when he shows his hand, laugh at him and say, "Get it fixed." Pull the chips into your bin. And then show your winning hand.

If it's a game like lowball and he says he has a seven, ask, "Seven what?"

Seven-five," he says hopefully.

"Seven-five-what?" you continue, letting out some more line.

"Seven-five-three-two-one," he says triumphantly, swallowing

*And when the game finally does break up and the poor soul is settling up, this is no time for compassion. This is the time to kick him in the face and scar him.*

the hook.

"No good; I've got a six."

If you ever make four-of-a-kind, never, never announce four-of-a-kind. Always say, "Two pair," and when your opponent reaches for the pot, add " ... of kings."

Once an opponent starts losing, step up the attack. Ask him what happened to all his chips. Tell him you've never seen him play so badly. Ask him if he's feeling OK. Warn him he's on tilt. Laugh when you beat him. Tell him you're going to take a trip to Mexico with his money. Suggest the stakes may be too high for him.

When he's losing badly, he's desperate to get even, and it's getting late, do everything you can to slow the game. Talk a lot. Rehash the prior hand interminably. Tell jokes. Create confusion. Constantly ask, "Who's it on?" "How much is the bet?" "Who raised?" "What's the game?" Take a very long time to shuffle the cards. Misdeal and start over a lot.

If you're playing in someone's home and the victim is the host, ask, "How come you have to clean the kitchen only when you're winning, Ralph?"

When he's thrashing about like a wounded bull, say, "I'm tired. Let's break the game up early tonight." This is guaranteed to send him over the edge.

And when the game finally does break up and the poor soul is settling up, this is no time for compassion. This is the time to kick him in the face and scar him. When the damage reports come in, say something like, "Boy, you really lost a lot of money tonight, didn't you?" Or, "I see you threw the party again."

If he writes a check and you get it, peer at it suspiciously and ask, "Is this check good?"

Finally, as he lurches out the door, be sure to yell, at the top of your lungs, "Tell 'em where you got it."

# POKER BOOKS THAT MADE ME QUAKE

**B**ad as it was, the 1994 Southern California earthquake at least did two good things for me. First, the shaking somehow managed to get my broken dishwasher working again. More important, it forced me to weed out a lot of useless poker books from my collection.

The quake toppled my wall unit, sending poker books, plants, stereo and computer components, bric-a-brac, and such priceless mementos as my bowling trophies into a tangled heap of broken glass and rubble. A few days later when the trembling had begun to die down (mine, not the earth's), I started the task of picking through the remains. I discovered a large number of weird and mainly useless books on poker that I hadn't looked at in years, some, decades. Some I barely remember buying; all I wished I hadn't.

I'm not talking, of course, about treatises by authors like Mike Caro, Mason Malmuth, and David Sklansky. I'm referring to all those overrated books that promise to turn you into a big winner overnight.

You see, my problem (OK, *one* of my problems) is that I'm gullible and easily manipulated. Most of the vast fortune I once had accumulated (OK, half-vast) has been drained by get-rich schemes, with the remainder being squandered on baldness cures and bad poker books.

Since I had fewer shelves remaining after the quake, and since I'd be embarrassed to be killed by these books in case they fell on me during an aftershock, I decided to do some judicious pruning.

The first book to go was called *Poker Secrets Exposed,* by Pee-Wee Herman.

Next to get tossed was a work with the intriguing title of *Outrageous Poker Plays: How to Get Away with Murder.* The authors were Erik and Lyle Menendez.

Another book I quickly dumped was *How to Knock Your Opponents Out of Tournaments* by Tonya Harding. Sure, Tonya Harding plays poker. Why do you think she's called the Queen of Clubs?

Then, I threw away a book on golf that had accidentally gotten mixed in with the poker stuff. It was written by Lorena Bobbitt and entitled *How to Correct Your Slice.*

After some thought, I also decided to discard that book about becoming a poker player, quitting your job, and sleeping until noon. While it has some good stuff in it, a lot of the advice has backfired on me. In the section on selecting desirable opponents, for example, it says you should seek out smokers and people with tattoos, because smokers lack self-control, and anyone who'd mutilate his body with a tattoo couldn't be very intelligent.

Great advice. All I got from playing with smokers was emphysema. And the last time I check-raised a player covered with tattoos, I got slugged. And *she* hit pretty hard, too.

Still another book to hit the trash chute was the one that promises a guaranteed income for life from poker, and espouses a lot of cute tricks, such as adding a submarine sandwich to the pot at home games to induce players to chase with weak hands. I think I once wrote about the one time I tried tossing a sub into the pot; Big Denny caught and swallowed it in midair.

I also got rid of all those books offering elaborate point-count systems for Omaha high-low. These books show you how to evaluate starting hands by assigning point values for each individual card, points for straight possibility cards, points for pairs, points for low hands, points for position, in fact, points for just about everything including the phases of the moon.

You need a doctorate in math and several minutes of calculation just to decide whether to play a hand. Who needs it? Who can remember it? I'm from the keep-it-simple school of poker. In fact, my fans will be happy to know that I am currently in the process of writing my own simplified poker books.

I'm doing a hold'em book that will consist of just three words: "Play big cards." The second book, on Omaha high-low, will be more comprehensive, consisting of *six* words: "Play big cards or little cards." I challenge anyone out there to prove that you need to know more than that.

Come to think of it, those are going to be the *only* books in my poker library of the future. It would sure make cleanup a lot easier after the next quake.

# SAVE THE DEALERS

The nasty issue of dealer abuse is a subject that sorely needs attention. It's a problem unique to poker and it won't be solved just by asking players to be nice.

I believe that more draconian methods are needed, and herewith offer a few practical ideas that casinos and cardrooms can implement to keep players in line and dealers in one piece.

*Discipline them:* Make offenders write "I will not blame the dealer" at least a hundred times on a blackboard.

*License them:* You have to get a license to drive a car, so why shouldn't players be required to get a license to play poker? To obtain such a license, every poker player would be required to pass a written exam that would include questions on proper behavior and decorum. (Such as the maximum distance cards may be thrown, for example.)

*School them:* This would be similar to sending bad drivers to traffic school. Should a player violate a casino's code of conduct, he would be issued a citation and his player's license would be revoked until he took a remedial course at a Bad Players School.

*Rehabilitate them:* More severe treatment might be needed for chronic offenders. These hard cases would be shipped to behavior-modification detention centers similar to the type that Red China once used to indoctrinate its non-conforming citizenry. But instead of chanting, "Chairman Mao is my friend," these wayward poker players would be forced to recite, "The dealer is my friend" all through the day. Then Leo Buscaglia (the love-cures-all psychologist) would hug them to pieces; diet/exercise guru Richard Simmons would ooze smarmy sympathy and understanding all over them; and Lawrence Welk's band would play bubble music around the clock. I guarantee that after two weeks of this treatment, even the most incorrigible psychopath would have his brain softened and would emerge just as sweet-tempered and benevolent as Mr. Rogers.

*Condition them:* In the famous Pavlovian response experiments, dogs were made to salivate when a bell rang because they had been conditioned to associate the bell with feeding time. Well, every time a player suffers a horrendous beat and merely murmurs, "nice hand" to his opponent, the dealer should ring a bell and reward him with a hot dog. After a time, he will come to associate the bell with civilized behavior.

*Shock them:* The opposite approach to conditioning therapy is aversion therapy, which is how they teach rats to negotiate a maze. First, hot-wire all the players' chairs. Then, when a player does something bad, the dealer can press a button to send him a nice shot of electricity. The voltage can be adjusted to reflect the seriousness of the offense, the number of times it has been committed, or simply to allow the dealer to vent his or her emotions over personal aggravations like a toothache or PMS.

*Whip them:* If a club is too penurious to install the necessary electrical wiring, it can save money by issuing whips to floormen. A few well-placed lashes across a miscreant's back should bring even the most dedicated troublemaker into line.

*Medicate them:* A licensed pharmacist should be on duty at each casino to prescribe an appropriate drug such as Valium, Halcion, lithium carbonate, or Prozac to calm unruly players. If the player won't cooperate and take his medication, it would be a simple matter to slip it to him in his food. If the drugs don't do the trick, a little lobotomy surgery might be in order. Some might consider this rather severe, but I think most dealers would approve.

*Nag them:* Bring in the player's mother to scold him and wash his mouth out with soap. This may be tough to do, however, if his mother is playing at the next table and behaving even worse than he is.

*Fine them:* This might be the most effective solution of all; it's what business management books call a win-win situation. Every time a player is abusive, fine him a set amount and hand over his confiscated chips to the dealer. For example, dock the player a dollar for cussing, a fiver for throwing cards, a ten-spot for throwing a lighted cigarette, three red chips for spitting saliva, a green chip for spitting tobacco juice, and a Franklin for choking the dealer into unconsciousness. This way the player gets to work off his aggression while the dealer gets to work up his bank account.

# THE PERILS OF THE NONSMOKER

## Part One: Light Up, Pardner — or Else

I am always astonished when smokers snarl at tourists who complain about having to inhale second-hand smoke. To me that's a little like a mugger getting mad when his victim screams. But I hadn't realized how bad the "smoker's rights" backlash had become until my last trip to Las Vegas.

There I was, playing poker and minding my own business, when a cowboy seated next to me fired up a Marlboro and enveloped me in smoke. As quietly as I could, I pulled out a small fan and turned it on.

Instantly an alarm sounded and bedlam erupted. Smokers shouted curses: "Health freak!" "Wussy!" "Pervert!" Two security guards ran up. They grabbed me under the arms and dragged me through the casino as players spat on me and pelted my head with ashtrays.

The guards carried me through a door that said, "Behavior Modification" and into a small room where they began to sing, "Smoke, smoke, smoke that cigarette," while beating out the tune on my ribs with rubber hoses.

When I regained consciousness, one of them, an immense creature named Bubba, asked, "Wheah you from, boy?"

"Los Angeles," I groaned.

"I knew it!" he yelled, whopping my right kidney.

"Wheah in Los Angeles?" demanded the other guard who had a sloped forehead and went by the name of Jim Bob.

"Well, uh, Hollywood ... sort of," I admitted.

"Hollywood!" Jim Bob assaulted my left side. I hoped my

kidneys weren't damaged. I was nearly tapped out at poker and had been thinking about selling one of them.

"Were you tryin' to make some kinda statement with that fan of yourn?" Bubba questioned.

"Hell, no," I replied. "I was just trying to breathe."

"Ah also seen you wavin' your hand around, boy."

"I wasn't protesting," I assured him. "I just wanted to cut a hole through the smoke so I could see my cards."

"We got good ventilation in that there room," Jim Bob said. "You just imagined theah was smoke."

"Oh, yeah? Then how come a woman passed out in the elevator last night from the fumes coming off my clothes?" A rain of blows indicated that my wisecrack was an error. Jim Bob offered me an unfiltered Camel. I shook my head.

"He's from L.A.," Bubba reminded him. "Them fellas don't smoke nothing but Virginia Slims. Look, boy, you're in Nevada now. Man's country. More people smoke heah than in another state, in case y'all didn't know."

"Sure. And Nevada happens to have the highest rate of cancer deaths from smoking."

"Don't mean nothing," Bubba scoffed. "Mah granny smoked three packs a day, dipped snuff, an' she lived to be 96."

"When she died, did you embalm her or hang her in the smokehouse?" Another bad error. I covered my head and kept talking. "Look guys. The chemicals in tobacco kill 400,000 Americans every year. It's not healthy to be around burning cigarettes. The EPA says passive smoke causes thousands of lung cancer deaths each year alone. As for heart disease ..."

"Don't the ERA pick up sick dawgs?" asked Bubba.

"That's the SPCA. EPA stands for Environmental Protection Agency."

"Buncha commies," growled Jim Bob. "Them boys once arrested

me an' mah pa for fishing in Lake Mead."

"Ain't illegal to fish there," said Bubba.

"We was usin' dynamite," said Jim Bob.

The guards turned back to me. "Look heah, why can't you let those good old boys get a little enjoyment from a cigarette?" asked Bubba.

"Enjoyment? They're hooked on a drug. I bet every one of those 'good old boys' tried to stop smoking one time or another and couldn't. Why should I suffer over their problem?"

Bubba laid a hand the size of a ham on my shoulder. "Let's be reasonable, son. No reason why folks who smoke and folks who don't can't get along peaceable like."

"They can smoke all they want," I agreed. "Just figure out a way so I don't have to breathe in that junk."

"Why don't y'all wear a gas mask?"

"Why don't they all wear diver's helmets?"

Suddenly the door burst open and another tourist was dragged in. Bubba asked what he'd done, and the new guard sneered.

"Caught him leavin' a table short while he tried to crawl outside for fresh air."

"OK," said Jim Bob. "Got no more time to waste with you. Gonna fit in with the other players, or would you druther me an' pa take you out on Lake Mead?"

I considered briefly. "Know where I can buy some Virginia Slims?"

# Part Two: The Controversy Continues

Where there's smoke, there's *ire,* because nothing ignites hostilities between poker players like the issue of cardroom smoke. The battle is as eternal and intense as the Hatfield and McCoy feud. One anti-smoker sent a letter to the *Card Player* threatening to spray pepper on offenders, while a smoking partisan darkly warned that Hitler got started by being intolerant of cigarette smoke.

Oddly, California recently banned smoking in state prisons. It's interesting to know that murderers and pickpockets are considered more worthy of protection than poker players.

Spitting on sidewalks used to be acceptable until it was found that doing so spread tuberculosis so the practice was prohibited. Well, they've found that smoking not only kills smokers but the people around them as well, so how come spitting got outlawed in all public places while smoking still hasn't?

I'll tell you why: Because there was no money to be made in spitting. If there were, manufacturers would have had a saliva lobby, just like the tobacco lobby. You'd have had calls for "spitter's rights," with saliva lobby spokesmen declaring, "No causal effect has been proven to link spitting to tuberculosis." And of course ads and billboards would have depicted spitting as glamorous, healthy, fun, and a neat way to expand your social circle.

No, it won't be easy to win the war and clear out cardroom smoke, even though the nonsmokers outnumber the smokers by roughly two-to-one. Harry Truman once said, "If you can't stand the heat get out of the kitchen." Today the war cry is, "If you can't stand the smoke, get out of the cardroom." Smoking activists constantly remind "whiners" that it's legal to light up in cardrooms ... meaning that the majority of us who don't smoke should just shut up and endure being annoyed and endangered by the minority who do.

I believe nonsmokers have the right to do whatever they can to change the situation. Personally, I'd like to see smokers forcibly restrained with the kind of mask they put on Hannibal the Cannibal. But you can't do that — yet.

Another thing you can't do is tell smokers their habit is bad for their health. They don't want to hear it. And you can't tell them their habit is bad for your health. They don't want to believe it.

It's human nature to resent facts that contradict one's beliefs or desires. Galileo got in hot water for saying the earth revolved around the sun. Ditto for Rachel Carson (author of *Silent Spring*) for warning that DDT was harmful. And today a hard core of skeptics won't admit that CFCs are depleting the ozone layer. I have a friend who thinks it's all a plot to make him buy a new radiator for his car.

So don't expect smokers to be swayed by the report of the Environmental Protection Agency stating that secondhand smoke kills 50,000 people a year. Similarly, don't hold your breath (literally and figuratively) expecting cardroom operators to ban smoking voluntarily — no more than the mayor of a resort town in the movie *Jaws* would close the beach and hurt tourist business just because of some alleged man-eating shark.

A few small things can be done to ward off cardroom smoke. A portable fan will deflect fumes and advertise your concern to smokers, most of whom try to be considerate. If you play at off-peak hours the air will be better. (I recommend Tuesdays, between 5:30 a.m. and 6:00 a.m.) If you can, move up to bigger games — you'll usually encounter fewer smokers. But these are just Band-Aid measures at best. After all, playing at a nonsmoking table is a little bit like swimming in the nonchlorinated end of a swimming pool.

So is there any hope for poker players who prefer clean lungs? Yes, lots. As the medical evidence against cigarette smoke mounts, social pressures are forcing laws that are making smokers the outcasts of the '90s.

Not so long ago, it was legal to smoke on planes, in theaters, in elevators, even in hospitals. No more. Today smoking is prohibited in many workplaces and government and public buildings. Numerous cities, including Los Angeles, have banned smoking in restaurants. We've come a long way from the time when cigarette ads featured actors in white coats pretending to be doctors and telling us which cigarette was healthiest for our throats.

But perhaps the best hope of all for us fresh-air fiends is a bill recently introduced in Congress by Henry Waxman (of Los Angeles, naturally) to prohibit smoking in all public buildings. If that passes, the game's over.

So if you want to light a candle rather than curse the smoke, take a minute to write your local and national legislators in support of anti-smoking bills. You just might breathe easier for doing so.

# Part Three: To Smoke or Not to Smoke

A miracle no less remarkable than Moses parting the Red Sea may be in the making. Smoking in all card casinos in California could be banned in a couple of years.

The strongest anti-smoking legislation in the country — a bill that prohibits smoking in virtually every workplace in the state — was passed by the California Assembly (no doubt in response to one of my anti-smoking columns). It took effect January 1, 1995, and was amended at the last minute to exclude bars and cardrooms. But provisions provide for monitoring and possible addition of those two venues as well a bit down the road.

Skeptics doubted the bill would ever pass because of the pervasive influence of the free-spending tobacco lobby. (A million-dollar "contribution" to lawmakers by cigarette interests is like a fifty-cent toke to you and me.)

But it became a new ball game when the EPA report on second-hand smoke came out.

If smoking is banned, just how will it affect players and cardrooms? For answers, I interviewed smokers, casino executives, psychologists, and other experts, and after extensive research developed the following scenario.

First of all, it will be a shock for players to walk in from the outside fresh air, expecting to be hit by a bracing wave of stale cigarette smoke, only to be greeted by ... more fresh air! To soften the impact, some clubs plan to install decompression chambers similar to those used by deep-sea divers. Players will enter a compartment filled with smoke, carbon monoxide, and similar deadly gases. They will be allowed to take a few calming deep breaths, and then the air gradually will be altered until it reaches that normal mixture of invisible, odorless, tasteless, life-giving oxygen and nitrogen that smokers find so unnatural.

It's like the old joke about people who grew up breathing Los Angeles smog: they don't trust air they can't see.

And what will happen to the cigarette girls? No longer will we hear their familiar lilting cry of, "Cigars, cigarettes." Instead they will be trilling, "Nicotine gum, nicotine patches, tranquilizers."

Pacifiers could become a big business. Just visualize a table full of burly louts sucking rubber nibs.

Chewing tobacco should be in big demand, and we may even see the return of spittoons. This is OK, unless you happen to be wearing white bucks ... or open-toed sandals.

Of course, none of this will ever satisfy hard-core smokers. They'll still need their constant fix, and at times there may be more players outside the club than inside. A full table will be as rare as a Hollywood virgin.

Especially hard hit will be the Asian games players, to whom smoking is as much a part of their ritual as banging on the table.

The clubs will find various ways to respond to short games. All the tables will change over to time collections, of course. They may charge an admission fee, forcing a player to pay each time he goes out and comes back in. In desperation, some clubs may simply install outdoor tables in the parking lot.

For dealers, a smoking ban would cut both ways. Short tables would mean smaller pots and fewer tips, but not having to breathe smoke might let them live long enough to collect their pensions.

For husbands who don't want wives to know they've played poker, life will be easier once they don't come home reeking of telltale fumes. I actually know of one player who wears disposable hospital pants and tops at the club, then throws them away and changes into street clothes when he goes home.

Much of my scenario is of course satirical. But I've been wary of joking about smoking ever since a reader responded to something I had written. His health had been ruined by cigarettes and he didn't think smoking was funny.

He's right — though he also should remember that humor can be a very potent weapon. The simple truth, to quote a slogan from a current campaign by the California Department of Health Services, is that "Smoking stinks."

If the smoking ban does pass, I honestly believe that smokers will adjust and nonsmokers will come more often and play longer in a much more enjoyable environment. Owners will make more money than ever and perhaps sleep better for knowing their establishments are no longer health hazards to their customers and employees.

# SECTION FOUR

## And the Losers Say, 'Deal!'

The Moving Finger writes; and having writ,
Moves on: nor all your piety nor wit
Shall lure it back to cancel half a line,
Nor all your tears wash out a word of it.
*Omar Khayyam*

(Translation: The floorman's decision is final.)
*Max Shapiro*

# FOLLOWING THE TOURNAMENT ELEPHANTS

There's an old joke about a guy who goes to the circus and runs into his friend Joe who's taken a job grooming the elephants. Joe sobs out a heartbreaking story about the horrors of having to care for and shovel up after the huge beasts. The guy asks why he doesn't quit and find a decent job.

"What!?" the friend exclaims. "And leave show biz?"

I went through much the same thing when a card casino offered me a job writing up its annual tournament series. What a dream assignment, I thought. A ringside seat at the hottest poker action in town, and I get paid, too!

I overlooked one small detail: most of the tournaments started in the evening and didn't end until the milkman was making his rounds.

Imagine staying up all night and then trying to write a snappy, lucid, entertaining report when you're so bleary-eyed and woozy you can barely see, much less make sense out of a scribbled mass of undecipherable words and symbols that pass as notes. At first I tried to record a precise description of every card of every hand in perfect sequence. The sequence was first to go. Then I left out the suits. After a while I wasn't sure what the final hands were, and in the end I was satisfied if I could just remember who won.

Hold'em was bad enough, but trying to follow stud, where they deal out about ninety six cards, was like trying to keep track of Liz Taylor's husbands — or O.J. Simpson's attorneys.

Then there was the business of not saying anything bad about anybody. As my readers well know, that's a tough habit for me to break. In my first report I wrote, "Bakersfield Bob viciously flung the cards at his despised foe and snarled, 'Eat my shorts, you scumsucking yurt.'" The casino's censors changed that to read, "'Nice hand, old man,' he said, graciously pushing the chips to his friendly rival."

And my task was not exactly eased by the players as I danced around the table trying to follow the action. Remarks ran to things like, "Move away from me, you're bringing me bad luck." Or, "You trying to look at my cards, boy?" One player actually had the nerve to tell me to get him a cup of coffee. Then he got mad and didn't tip me when I forgot the cream. So you can guess what happened when I ask some grouchy pro, steaming after getting knocked out of the tournament by an amateur's miracle catch, to please turn over his losing hole cards for my write-up.

Even the spectators got on my case. "Move out of the way so I can see, you baldheaded baboon," was one of the more printable comments from the yahoos in the gallery.

But the worst part was the hours. After finally completing a report that I could only hope was remotely coherent, I would stagger out of the casino into the blinding sunlight, lurch around the parking lot looking for my car, then steer onto the freeway into morning rush hour and pray I'd make it home without weaving into oncoming traffic. After a couple of weeks of this torture, I began to wish that I would hit oncoming traffic and end my misery.

Then I'd finally get home and decide to eat something. Was I supposed to eat dinner or breakfast? I didn't know. Then I'd remember that I hadn't shopped for days — no time or energy — and I'd end up choking down some stale pizza or some other equally unpalatable leftover.

And what fun it is going to bed at 10 a.m., trying to ignore bright daylight, barking dogs, garbage trucks, and your resentment at the guy who didn't tip you because you forgot his cream. The first day of my "dream" assignment I finally dropped off into a fitful doze about noon, only to be jolted awake by some salesman calling to sell me a timeshare in Barstow. I ripped out the phone and threw it into the closet. When I got to the club that night the first person I ran into was Action Al. "Been trying to call you all day," he complained. I wanted to come over to pay back that hundred I owe you ... but I lost it playing Omaha." Like it's my fault.

One last thing. To kill time while waiting for the final table to materialize, I'd play poker — and lose, of course. As I neared the end of my ordeal, my blood pressure was sky high, my ears were ringing, my hands shook uncontrollably, my vision had become blurred, my speech slurred, and I'd lost $400 more than I've earned.

But hey, that's show biz.

*Somehow, I don't think this is the job I signed up for.*

# BRAIN POWER PILLS
# FOR OMAHA PLAYERS

S ome time ago, *Playboy* magazine (I buy it only to read the jokes and get material for my own articles) had an article on "smart drugs." These are an array of high-powered pharmaceuticals, vitamins, and nutrients that are gulped down by hip people looking to enhance their IQs and cognitive abilities. The rage of the 90s, we are told.

Steroids for the mind! Brain boosters to give you the power of a 586 computer! Instantly, I knew. This was *it*. The magic bullet, the poker elixir I had been seeking for years.

I located one of the smart bars pushing this stuff, a place called Phi Beta Kaplan. Right away I knew I was in the right place. People were wearing Mensa sweatshirts and doing crossword puzzles with pens. One man was reading a Mason Malmuth book as though he actually understood it. The blonde behind the juice bar wore a name tag that read, "Brainy Janie." I asked her if she had smart pills to help my poker game.

"Oh, yes," she said brightly. "Many poker players come here. Matter of fact, Big Denny is our best customer."

"Really?" What kind of pills does he eat?"

"Oh, he doesn't care, so long as they're chocolate-coated."

"Well, what kind would you suggest?"

She consulted a handbook. "Depends on your game. With seven-card stud, for example, you want to recall the open cards. So we recommend our 'elephant memory' pill, which is loaded with memory enhancers like hydergine, B-12, and choline."

"Sounds impressive," I said. "What else you got?"

"Well, if you play no-limit hold'em, you need to remain calm and resolute. We recommend tryptophan, which the brain uses to produce a relaxant endorphin called serotonin."

I was getting excited. This lady knew her stuff. "What do you have for Omaha high-low?"

Brainy Janie looked at me ... differently. "I can't help you," she finally sniffed.

"Why not?"

"Well, for one thing, any dosage strong enough to help an Omaha high-low player would probably be lethal."

A tear rolled down my cheek. We Omaha players get nothing but abuse.

"Look," Brainy Janie said more kindly, "why don't you consider aversion therapy? A few shock treatments will make you forget all about that stupid game."

"That 'stupid game' is the future," I replied haughtily. "It will change our lives."

"So will the hole in the ozone layer. Have you thought about joining Omaholics Anonymous?"

"No!" I shouted. "I'm an Omaha player and I'm not ashamed of it. Will you help me or not?"

The brain lady gave up. "OK, I'll give it a try." She turned to the Omaha section in her handbook. "It says Omaha players like to be in every hand and can't stand to sit one out. Is this true?"

I nodded my head eagerly. Brainy Janie took some containers off a shelf and spooned powder into a blender.

"What's that?" I asked

"Caffeine and Ritalin — stimulants. They'll make you so hyped up and jittery you'll *never* be out of a hand."

I smiled broadly, and she continued to read. "It says Omaha addicts would rather play than eat. OK, let's throw in some 'phets for appetite suppression."

I began to jump up and down, clapping my hands in glee. "More! More!" I beseeched her.

"This can't be true!" she suddenly exclaimed. "It says Omaha high-low players routinely chase straight draws, even when pairs and three-flushes hit the board."

I blushed. "We try to forget the board. Otherwise, we'd have to fold too many hands."

Janie signed and dropped in a handful of cannabis. "That should take care of the old memory cells. What else?"

"One more thing," I confessed. "No matter what we have, we always get beat by the last card in Omaha. That's when we have tantrums and yell and scream and throw our porridge on the floor. That's the yummy, fun part."

Janie looked up "masochistic highs" in her book. "Well, amino acids like phenylalanine and tyrosine in large doses can cause irritability. Let's add 25,000 milligrams of each. And that should complete the formula."

So saying, she blended the ingredients, ran the mixture through a machine, and out came a stream of bright yellow tablets.

I was awe-struck. Smart pills to enhance the pleasure of Omaha high-low. "What do you call them?" I asked.

She showed me the label: "Dumb Pills."

# DON'T WORRY; PLAY HAPPY

**M**y game needed a tune-up. Make that a major overhaul. I'd made more bank withdrawals in a month than John Dillinger did in his whole career But I didn't want to tax my brain with technical stuff. I mean, when David Sklansky tells you to try to think what your opponent thinks you think he thinks you have, my head hurts. I have trouble just figuring out what I think *I* have.

No, this is the age of quick fixes. Why bother to diet and exercise when there's liposuction? Why go into therapy for a dozen years when you can just pick a slogan from some self-help book: *I'm OK, You're OK, Give Yourself a Kiss* ... whatever works. Today there's a slogan for *every* situation. My favorite is Nike's ad campaign theme: "Just do it." *Do what?* They never tell you. But as soon as I find out what it is I'm supposed to do, I'm certainly going to do it.

Never mind, there had to be a magic bullet somewhere to straighten out my play. So I read something written by Roy West. As usual, his title, in its entirety, consists of two words. These were: "Play happy."

Now there's a boy who makes sense. I think. Play happy and play well. Bingo, that's it! So I get a happy night's sleep, eat a big, happy breakfast, meditate with "Play happy" as a mantra, and happily read a scrapbook of my old columns. By noon the sun is shining, the birds are singing and I'm as happy as can be.

Happily, I head down the Hollywood Freeway and turn on the news. Another third-stage smog alert; breathing is not recommended. The drought is critical; we are rationed to one flush a day. Crime is up; the stock market is down. And scientists predict a major quake will soon kill everyone in L.A.

My smile fades a bit; I change stations. Nothing but rock and rap. Damn, don't they play Perry Como any more? I switch back to the news. Great! Major freeway tie-up ahead.

I get to the club two hours late with a steaming radiator. Inside, there's a long waiting list. The jackpot has just been cracked and lowered to a measly thirty dollars. I stifle a scream. "Play happy, play happy," I begin chanting to myself.

I finally get called. I walk to the table and am horrified to see my nemesis, Action Al. As hyper as a jackrabbit on speed, Action Al always manages to elevate my blood pressure.

"Here comes the rock," he chirps.

I start to snarl, "Hello, Al, how'd you get past the security guards?" But I remind myself, "Gotta play happy."

All the other players are downers, too. Grumpy Joe, who only speaks in poker clichés, has just lost another pot. "You only play the nuts, don't you?" he complains for the tenth time that day. "That's the last time I'm showing you second best."

Big Denny, who owns a sleazy used-car lot with the famous "fifty-fifty" guarantee — fifty seconds or fifty feet, whichever comes first — rakes in the pot with one hand and stuffs a whole bag of potato chips in his mouth with the other. I turn green, then greener as some clod next to me fires up an enormous pipeful of Cap'n Jack's Navy Cut Tire Shavings.

I decide to watch the action and just wait for my blind. Ralph the Rattler, so named because he has more moves than a snake, shakes his head mournfully at the board as he checks.

A prune-faced old biddy stares at him suspiciously. Finally, she bets.

The Rattler raises.

The biddy curses murderously and throws her cards at him.

Ugly Ed the dealer, who hasn't been tipped a nickel by this table, warns the biddy about throwing cards and she curses him, too.

My heart is palpitating and I'm beginning to sweat. "Play happy! Play happy!" I'm chanting to myself furiously.

Dirty Wally spots me and comes over. In excruciating detail, he describes his last forty bad beats. A large wet spot spreads where his tears splash on the table. A fight breaks out as Action Al and the old biddy wrestle for a "lucky seat" someone has vacated. Finally the O.B. sinks a bony elbow in Action Al's gut and primly sits down.

"Change the deck!" someone screams after each hand. "Change the dealer!" someone always screams back.

"Service!" bellows big Denny. "Can't you get any service in this lousy place!"

My ears are ringing, and I'm getting a headache.

Suddenly, a terrible commotion breaks out. Distracted by all the noise, Ugly Ed has neglected to burn a card, the old biddy bets out with a whoop, and Big Denny, who knows his nut flush has been beaten by a full house, is threatening to sit on the dealer's head. Finally a floorman is called. He rules that since action was accepted, the card plays. Big Denny threatens to sit on *his* head.

By now my chest hurts, I'm dizzy, I want to kill everybody at the table, and I haven't even put in an ante yet.

"You're the big blind," Ugly Ed politely informs me.

"Get it fixed!" I yell at him.

I storm out to the parking lot and discover my battery is dead and there's a big dent in my fender.

There's only one way you can possibly play poker happy, I've decided, and that's to carry around a big tank of laughing gas.

# I GOTTA DO COMEDY ...

Playing poker can send you soaring one day and crashing the next, and so can writing a poker column.

The other day, I was playing my favorite game, Omaha high-low and winning big. I had $1 chips piled up to my clavicle. A young woman wandered over to watch this curious game. Her eyes widened as she spotted my impressive stacks. "Let me stand behind him," she cooed. "He looks like the real expert."

My heart fluttered. I reached under my cushion for one of the twenty copies of *Card Player* magazine I always keep there. "Here," I said as casually as I could. "Read my column?"

"You write a poker column?" she asked in awe. "I knew I picked the real expert." She read, laughing at my witticisms and "hmmming" at my profundities.

"Let me autograph that for you," I offered. "Maybe I could give you some poker lessons some time."

At that point, her boyfriend walked up. He had a bushy beard and looked as if he just dropped out of a tree. My libido cooled, but not my euphoria. What a life, I thought. Me, a poker celebrity.

A few nights later, I was at the same table, losing big. I needed pumping up. I turned to my friend, Benny. "Read my last column?" I asked brightly.

"You call that a column?"

"What was wrong with it?" I asked indignantly. The column consisted of advice for staying off tilt. I thought it was pretty good, a classic, a lifetime of experience crammed into a single, priceless article.

"Get to sleep the night before? Eat food? You call that a column?" Benny dismissed me with a derisive snort and turned back to his bowl of matzoh ball soup. "Maybe some of it seemed obvious," I answered weakly, "but all of it works."

I looked down at my chips and noticed they were a quart low. I pulled out another Franklin. How could I be losing so much in this game? Gotta tighten up. I felt the first faint stirrings of panic. Could I, of all people, be going on tilt?

A woman with ten pounds of jewelry sat down on my right. She was raising every hand — on nothing. A feeding frenzy developed. I got pulled into every hand, just enough to call, never enough to win. My head buzzed. I hadn't gotten enough sleep the night before. My stomach started churning. I hadn't eaten since breakfast. I kept losing. I was going in with junk and paying off rocks who hadn't bet a number-two hand since Truman was president.

I was doing everything I said not to do in my column. Desperately, I tried to remember what I wrote. I tried to cool my fevered, raging brain. I began chanting mantras, picturing flickering candle flames. "Wait for the wave, wait for the wave," I started mumbling, trying to visualize waiting for a wave (hand) big enough to ride.

My playing got worse and my wallet got thinner. I was down almost a month's mortgage. Finally, an absolutely humongous pot began building. Eventually, six of us went all in. Even with just half the pot, my high hand could recoup a big percentage of my losses, and I had the top set of jacks on fourth street, with a straight working, yet. A third spade fell. I did make a ten-high flush, but hardly expected it to hold up. It didn't. I was beaten in two places.

Long, long past my predetermined quitting time, I rose shakily and went home. I was shattered out of a fitful sleep at 11 the next morning. My editor. "Where's next week's column?" she demanded.

"I've already got one column in," I reminded her.

"Which one was that?"

"Omaha high-low."

"We're not using it."

"Why not?" I shouted.

"Omaha high-low isn't a real game."

"The hell it isn't," I yelled back. "Lots of clubs offer it now. And that was a great column, maybe the best I've written so far. It was the definitive piece on how to play Omaha high-low."

My editor was unimpressed. "You're not supposed to write serious stuff," she said crushingly. "We've got real poker players for that. We hired you to do funny stuff, you know, ha-ha experiences of the little guy."

"Little guy!" I sometimes get up to $5-$10. So that's it. Nobody gives a rat's tail for my poker savvy. They want laughs. But what's so funny about poker? What's funny about losing my month's mortgage payment? OK. You want funny? I'll give you funny. Change my byline to Slapsy Maxie Shapiro. Paint a Groucho mustache and glasses on my pictures. No, hold the mustache — I already have one. Just give me a funny hat and send me out to the poker tables to write about how funny it is to lose to people who can't play half as well as I can but are just luckier.

You want poker funny? Here's poker funny.

A guy hears a friend of his has taught his dog to play poker. He goes over to his friend's house and, sure enough, there's his friend and the dog playing two-handed poker. The dog is doing everything. He's betting, raising, calling, asking for cards by slapping his paw on the table, even dealing when it's his turn.

The guy is astounded. "That must be the smartest dog in the world," he exclaims.

"He's not that smart," the owner replies. "The jerk keeps drawing two to a flush."

What a tragedy. I spend weeks doing the math to answer one of the world's most important questions — The odds of having an ace-deuce without a back-up card, come in for the nut low in Omaha.

Well, faithful reader, you'll never know now. I gotta do comedy.

# CHECKING OUT IN STYLE

I have a friend named Henry who I sometimes take hikes with. The other day, he surprised me by saying that I was one of about sixty acquaintances to whom he planned to leave $100 in his will. He wanted each of us to spend the cash on a good dinner.

Now, that's a classy thing to do. I've never been in anyone's will before, and even though Henry's a really nice guy, I can't wait for him to die so I can collect the $100 and enjoy a feast in his honor.

I started thinking about doing something similar, except that most of my friends would have trouble spending $100 in the places they eat. That's because the top price is usually about $4.95.

I've got a better idea. I think I'll leave each of my pals $40 for a buy-in to the $4-$8 Omaha high-low game ($35 for Short-Buy Woody). But to collect, they have to first come to my funeral. Otherwise, you give money to a poker player and you'll never see him again.

Once I got to thinking about it, I began to fantasize about custom-designing my whole funeral in a poker theme. Wouldn't that be fun? It might even get me a few lines in the *Los Angeles Times*.

Let's see … To start with, I don't want any of that somber funeral music. I want them to play Kenny Rogers' theme song, "The Gambler." That'll liven things up. I'd like the ushers to wear string ties and dealer name tags, and the rabbi to wear an eye shade over his *yarmulke*. Maybe the people from the Bicycle Club Casino could even lend me a couple of dance hall girls from the old Diamond Jim Brady festivities.

To make folks feel at home, you know, as though they were in a cardroom, I'd like lots of cigarette smoke blown into the room. Everyone will have his or her initials posted on a sign-up board in front, and mourners will have to be called before they are seated.

Of course, I'll write the eulogy myself. Otherwise, there'll just be a lot of pious platitudes that no one will listen to or believe. I'll throw in some good jokes. I have lots of snappy openers. How about, "Max folds." Or, "How's *this* for a bad beat, folks?" Or, "I see Max is drawing dead again."

Well, maybe those are a little too flippant. I guess I'll go with something more dignified, like, "Max Shapiro has gone to that Big Poker Game in the Sky."

Then the rabbi could read passages from some of my funnier articles. Not the Big Denny pieces, though. He would run up and overturn my casket. Of course, he might do it anyway.

Then some of the mourners could offer a few words. I can pretty much guess what they'll say.

Dirty Wally: "Let me tell you about some of *my* bad beats."

Ralph the Rattler: "I'd like to invite everyone to a game at my house tonight."

Big Denny: "When do we eat?"

I'd like to be laid out in my working clothes, the way my friends remember me best: grungy wash pants, card club T-shirt and cap (matching if possible; this is a formal funeral, after all), and the imitation polyester jacket I got from the old Hilton cardroom for putting in twenty hours of play.

In one hand I'd like to be clutching my favorite Omaha high-low starting hand — ace-ace-deuce-trey double suited. In my other hand, put a portable fan to blow away the cigarette smoke that probably killed me in the first place.

After they lower me into the ground, I'd prefer they dispense with the icky custom of having each mourner throw a shovelful of dirt in my face, much as they'll like to. Instead, I'd like my friends each to throw in a couple of poker chips. No fifty-cent chips, please. If I know Action Al, he'll throw in an IOU ... or maybe a check. Screaming Susan can throw cards, just as she does at the club.

Finally, for my grave marker, I'd like a heart, a spade, a diamond, and a club in each corner, with the emblem of a joker in the middle. The inscription will be quite simple — just the dates of my birth and death, and this epitaph: "Deal me out for a while."

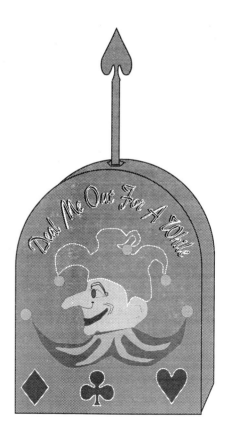

# IS THIS OMAHA OR IS THIS MARS?

**W**ere it not for jackpot poker, today we might be a colony of Mars. (I read this in the *National Enquirer*, so it must be true.)

It seems Commander 2311 and Ensign 2312, back from a reconnaissance mission to Earth, were reporting to their Martian president.

"Were the natives not startled by your tentacles and two heads?" the president asked.

"We were in California, Excellency," replied 2311, "and thus attracted no special attention. To blend in, we wore Bart Simpson T-shirts and traveled by skateboard. Everyone said we looked cool."

"We came across one of our countrymen on Earth," piped up Ensign 2312. I asked him his name and he said it was '5684.' I said, 'That's funny, you don't *look* Jewish.'"

The president of Mars lashed 2312 with his tentacles. "You have been warned about your corny Jewish Martian jokes," he fumed. Turning back to Commander 2311, he asked, "What do people in California do with their time?"

"They have vast Temples of Poker," said 2311.

"By Zeus, they share our religion!"

Commander 2311 shook his heads. "But they practice poker in a heathen way. They have a ritual they call Omaha high and low."

"Omaha what?" thundered the president.

"High and low, Lordship. You are dealt four cards with five in the middle. You play two cards in your tentacle for low, two for high; a low hand must not exceed an eight ..."

The president shut his ear flaps. "I cannot listen to this blasphemy. This is even worse than a new game our people are starting to play called *spit in outer space.*"

Commander 2311 rolled his six eyes. "There is more, Beloved Leader. People in California worship jackpots."

Steam escaped from the nostrils atop the two heads of the President of Mars. "What is 'jackpots'?"

"Well, they use little wheels called chips ..."

"I was in a delicatessen when they sold little wheels," interrupted Ensign 2312. "A woman said they were 'bagels.'" I ate one and she asked me how I liked it. 'Delicious,' I said. 'I bet they would taste great with lox and cream cheese.'"

*"That does it!"* bellowed the president. "That joke is older than Johnny Moss." He fired his blaster and 2312 fell to the ground moaning and laughing.

Commander 2311 continued. "The little wheels are equal in value to one of our credits. In their game of five and ten hold'em, they drop two credits in a jackpot slot each hand, about sixty an hour, until someone wins all the wheels."

"Sixty credits an hour," marveled the president. "That would buy a lot of lottery tickets. Is it hard to make a jackpot?"

"Aces that are full must be beaten by four-of-a-kind."

The Martian leader punched some buttons on one of his foreheads, but nothing happened. "Great Spock, my memory board cannot even compute this great number. Well, I deserve as much for buying it at a swap meet. If these cards ever appear, is the jackpot then given to him with the greater hand?"

"No, Your Worship. It is divided into parts of four, and he with the lesser hand is awarded three of the four parts."

The president scowled. "Surely thou art putting me on."

"No, Excellency. And in pursuing jackpots, the people pay no heed to how poker should be observed. They will call thrice-raised pots cold with a pair of deuces; they will always play an ace and any other card, though even the suits be dissimilar."

"Sinful," whispered the president. "Tell me more about jackpots."

"At sundown, a great commotion arises when new jackpot totals are posted in the temple. Half the worshippers say hosannas while the others bitch mightily at the numbers. But the worst I have not yet told. You have heard of the Russian scientist Pavlov?"

"Yes," said the president. "He fed dogs and rang a bell at the same time. Then he just rang a bell but the dogs would still salivate. Pavlovian response."

"Exactly. Well, the high priests at the Temples of Poker have conditioned worshippers in just such a sadistic manner. From time to time they will sound a gong to proclaim double jackpots. And then an awful spectacle occurs. The players drool and slobber like rabid dogs. They cry, 'Jackpot! Jackpot!' and beat noisily upon the tables. They beseech the dealers to deal them a jackpot, making intemperate offers — half their winnings, their wives, their firstborn. It is terrible to behold."

"You have done well, Commander," said the president. "We will seal off Earth forever lest these fanatics from California infect our people with their cockamamie worship of jackpots." He hesitated. "One final question."

"Yes, Your Grace?"

"Can you tell me more about this game they call Omaha high and low?"

# A LITTLE RESPECT, PLEASE

A scene in a movie called *The Treasure of the Sierra Madre* and a passage from a James Bond novel called *Casino Royale* have stuck in my mind over the years. Both, I think, have relevance to conduct at the poker table.

In the film, a grizzled old prospector and two partners find gold in the mountains of Mexico. When the vein plays out, the old man asks his friends to help him fill in the trenches they've dug. A cynical Humphrey Bogart says why bother. "This mountain's been good to us," the old man replies. "The least we can do is leave her the way we found her."

In the novel, James Bond beats the villain out of a zillion francs in a baccarat game. Euphoric, he is tempted to celebrate by plastering chips all over the roulette table, but thinks better of it; he senses that such a gauche act would be repaying Lady Luck with a slap in the face.

In both instances, the heroes are driven by a code of honor and are showing respect to some mysterious force that has favored them. Call it decency, call it karma, call it superstition if you will. Just remember what Doyle Brunson once said: "There are bigger faults than superstitions."

I'm not asserting that a poker god exists and that he (she?) will reward you if you play like a lady or a gentleman and obey all the unwritten rules of poker conduct. What I am saying is that it doesn't hurt to act as if your actions *are* being judged ... somewhere. As they say, what goes around comes around. And what's wrong with just trying to make the damn game as pleasant as possible for everyone at the table?

My own conduct is not always impeccable. I get tired, frustrated, and provoked like anyone else. And my code of ethics does not extend to Ralph the Rattler, who I think is fair game for anything you can do to him. But in general, I try to treat the game and the players with the same deference and respect that I would like to be shown.

I am appalled by players who try to intimidate everyone at the table with loud, boorish, or eccentric behavior (and by those writers who say it's good strategy). Hey, guys, cut the crap and just play poker, OK?

I never in my life have asked for a change of cards. I don't want to delay the game. I don't need to call attention to my bad luck. And, if that's how the poker gods want the cards to fall, why should I risk offending them by challenging their judgment? I would never dream of coffee-housing by making phony comments about my hand, or yelling for the board to pair when I'm trying to make a flush. It's one thing to hesitate a tick before betting. But please, don't make a production out of it. Don't stare at the cards for two minutes before raising. You're not fooling anyone.

If you're out of a hand, don't talk loudly or comment on the action in progress. If a pair of fives flop, and you threw away the other two, don't moan until the hand is over.

If a player is a novice, or has a difficult decision to make, be patient and give him time to think. On the other hand, don't delay the game yourself. Pay attention. Know when it's your turn to act, and don't wait until then to recheck your hole cards. If you want to drink yourself into a fog, please do so at the bar, not at the table.

Don't fold out of turn, and when you do fold, don't show your cards (with players left) or throw them.

Tip the dealer. Like it or not, that's how cardrooms have structured pay scales to see that dealers get compensated beyond their minimum wage. Show some class. Don't be a deadbeat and force other players to carry your tipping load.

Don't make any cute moves, like reaching for your chips in hopes of stopping another player from betting. Don't slow-roll anyone or announce you have two pair ... of kings.

Don't constantly leave the game short by wandering around the casino.

One more thing. Regularly, we are told not to criticize the play of tourists — a move that will drive them away. This sounds fine on the surface, but I'm bothered by the underlying concept that recreational players are simply livestock to be held in a pen until they can be butchered. Some low-limit regulars, who think of themselves as elitist "pros," live in ratty apartments, drive old clunkers, and have little interest in life beyond gambling, while their disdained "prey" is likely to be a successful, happy, family man, and a better human being in every possible way.

The bottom line, then, is to respect the game, respect the players and maybe — maybe — the poker gods will respect you.

# MOZART GOES TO OMAHA

**A** recent news story said that listening to Mozart can make you smarter. Researchers at the Center for the Neurobiology of Learning and Memory at a California college found that students who listened to a Mozart piano sonata for ten minutes raised their tested IQ eight or nine points. The researchers suggested that complex classical music, by "reinforcing certain complex patterns of neural activity," might enhance abstract reasoning, such as that involved in mathematics and chess.

Could this work for poker as well? All of my previous experiments with gimmicks like mantras and smart drugs had ended disastrously, but Mozart seemed worth a shot. The study warned that the jump in IQ dissipated within fifteen minutes, but I figured that all I had to do was to keep listening continuously while I played cards.

So out I went to find some Mozart tapes. Now, I hadn't been in a record store since 1957, when I went to buy "Mule Train" by Frankie Laine, and I was amazed at the changes. The store didn't carry a single 33 1/3 rpm record! And the bands it featured ... The Enemas, Ingrown Toenail, Blood Transfusions. I didn't know whether I was in a record shop or a hospital emergency room.

I asked a bubble-headed salesgirl for classical records, and she stared at me blankly. "Classical? Like, you mean like The Rolling Stones, like?"

I finally located, at a markdown rack, a single classical cassette titled *Mozart's Greatest Hits*. It had things like fugues and sonatas. I had no idea what fugues and sonatas were, but I couldn't have cared less. I'd listen to twelve straight hours of The Enemas if it made me play smarter poker.

Armed with my secret weapon, I drove to a casino, put my name up for Omaha high-low, loaded ol' Wolfgang Amadeus into a cassette player, and pushed the play button. Instantly my ears were flooded with magical sounds. Harpsichords, flutes, French horns, and violins melded and wove complex and insinuatingly beautiful melodies. I felt my cerebral cortex warm as billions of dormant neural synapses flared to life. My IQ rose like a thermometer in the tropics, and intricate Omaha strategies began forming in my brain.

My name was called. I confidently strode to a table, sat down to wait for my blind, and alertly studied my typical Omaha opponents: slack-jawed, empty-eyed mouth-breathers.

I observed as a player with ace-deuce caught two low cards on the flop, then helplessly watched a king and queen follow. No low. The next hand, he held ace-deuce again, flopped the nut low, and got counterfeited on the river. The third hand, his nut low held up, but two other players also had ace-deuce, and he got one-sixth of the pot. The player, who happened to be a nuclear physicist, began drooling and calling for his mommy.

It was the same story all around the table. There were rocket scientists, heart surgeons, university professors — all had crumbled under a succession of Omaha bad beats and were carrying on and playing like lobotomized monkeys.

Suddenly, in my enlightened state, it all became clear to me. People weren't idiots to play Omaha; they *became* idiots from playing Omaha. Now I knew why America was dumbing down, why SAT scores were plummeting, why Beavis and Butthead were folk heroes, and why the caliber of our leaders had free-fallen from Thomas Jefferson to Dan Quayle.

Omaha has been killing off our brain cells! The game probably was brought here by the commies during the cold war to destroy us. I tried to flee, then realized something was wrong. My tape had ended ten minutes earlier! The Mozart effect was wearing off, my neurons were shutting down, and my IQ was now sinking like a thermometer in the Arctic. Frantically, I tried to reset the tape, but it was too late.

Before I knew what I was doing, I had put in my blind and picked up my cards. I held 2-3-7-9 offsuit. My only prayer was for an ace to hit the board. Two players raised, so I knew all the aces were out. But I was seized in the grip of Omaha madness. "Cap it!" I screamed. Lunacy, but who cared? I was playing Omaha.

I managed to get the tape going again, but it was no contest; Mozart didn't stand a chance against Omaha. It's just a good thing the game wasn't around two hundred years ago. If Mozart had played Omaha, he'd never have been able to write anything more complex than *How Much is That Doggie in the Window?*

# LET'S BUILD A STATUE

The movie *Godfather II* contains a poignant scene in which a Meyer Lansky-type character complains that Las Vegas has never acknowledged its debt to the man who was responsible for building a gambling mecca in the middle of a desert: Benjamin "Bugsy" Siegel.

Do you know, the mob figure says, shaking his head, that to this day there is not even a statue of this man anywhere in that town?

Well, *Godfather II* came out about twenty years after Mr. Siegel's sudden demise. Another twenty years has now gone by, and there still is no statue. I'd like to know why.

Oh, sure, Las Vegas is touchy about its past. "Gangsters, what gangsters? We're all corporate businessmen here."

We know that, but we also know that isn't the way it was in the beginning. And as Balzac said, "Behind every great fortune lies a great crime."

Anyway, with the passage of time, people who were once criminal outcasts become fondly remembered as merely colorful rogues. Pirates, highwaymen, cattle rustlers, smugglers — they're all been softened now by history and enshrined in local folklore.

And so it should be with Ben Siegel. And now that we've had the movie *Bugsy* that focused new interest on his life, this might be a good time to recognize what hath Ben wrought, and to credit him with being a visionary as well as a gangster.

An epilogue to *Bugsy* reminds us that the town that Siegel started when he built its first modern hotel for $6 million ($5 million over budget) today has annual revenues that approach the federal budget. Surely the man who dreamed all this up deserves some recognition.

I mean, without him, all those millions of tourists flocking in from Des Moines and Bakersfield would have no place to go for excitement except the local Elks Club to play $1 limit poker.

Other places erect statues in homage to their founders. Pennsylvania has statues of William Penn. Gettysburg has one of J. Paul Getty. Sydney, Australia, honors its founder, Sydney Plotkin. Romulus and Remus were only the mythological founders of Rome, but still rate a statue. Vegas has a real founder, and it won't even spring for a plaque.

For all tourists know, Las Vegas could have been invented by Walt Disney. Or Tinkerbell.

Australia takes a perverse pride in being settled by exiled convicts. The inhabitants of Pitcairn Island don't mind that they're descended from mutineers of the British ship Bounty. So why should Las Vegas' good citizens turn their backs on their patriarch just because he needed to kill a few people in his line of work?

After all, as Bugsy used to reassure people, "We only kill each other."

How much could a statue cost, anyway? With what they take in today, casinos could skim — I mean allocate — enough money in a few minutes to build a monument bigger than the Great Pyramid. And instead of being a turnoff, the statue could be a great tourist attraction.

Can't you see it now? A giant, welcoming statue of Bugsy towering astride the strip, a leg on each side, like the Colossus at Rhodes, or the Gateway Arch in St. Louis. In one hand, he extends a pair of dice. In the other, he points a .38. For added verisimilitude, we could riddle the sculpture with bullet holes.

Make it big enough, like the Statue of Liberty, and you could hollow it out and charge people admission to walk inside for an exhibit of Bugsy's life. In this display case, young Bugsy's first set of brass knuckles. On that wall, a photograph of the first candy store he knocked over. On that pedestal, the first bucket of cement he poured around someone's feet.

The statue could be a real money-maker. The souvenir shop alone would rake in a fortune. Founding Father T-shirts with a police mug shot of Bugsy would be a big seller. How about toy Tommy guns and blackjacks for the kiddies? Or maps showing where Bugsy's friends are buried out in the desert?

But profit should not be the motive. This statue must be erected to recognize the contribution of a man who did a lot more for this country than most of our presidents. I mean, tell me the truth, who left a greater legacy for America, Millard Filmore or Bugsy Siegel?

It is time for Las Vegas to shake off its paranoia, accept its heritage, and embrace the visionary who conjured an Arabian Nights fantasy out of barren desert sand.

# I'VE FOUND MY FINAL HOME

**C**ard Player magazine was planning to print an anthology of all the best stuff that's appeared in its pages during its first five years. The editor sent a letter to contributors asking if we had any special or favorite articles we'd like to have considered for possible inclusion.

Oh, sure, I've got lots of favorite articles I've written. Unfortunately, all of them were rejected. And for really stupid reasons, too. You know, like just because they were obscene, sexist, ethnically insulting, inaccurate, politically incorrect, libelous, or simply so offensive they would have caused readers to cancel their subscriptions or major advertisers to cancel their ad programs.

Big deal. They were funny; who cares about the rest? Maybe I'll publish my own anthology called *The Worst of Max Shapiro.*

Anyway, I leafed through my scrapbook of articles that were sanitized enough to make print, looking for any "favorites." What an inane request. All my stuff is brilliant! It's like asking Leonardo da Vinci to choose between the "Mona Lisa" and "The Last Supper." But then I came across one that did have special significance because it was so prophetic.

Some time ago, I wrote a piece about how I was going to design my own funeral in a poker theme. You know, have the ushers wear dealer's string ties, give the rabbi an eye shade to put over his *yarmulke*, play Kenny Rogers' "Know when to hold 'em, know when to fold 'em" song, have the mourners throw poker chips into my grave, that sort of fun stuff.

And the epitaph on my grave marker would read, "Deal me out for a while." (I always tear up when I read that line.) Of course I wrote that all in jest, or so I thought. I mean, I liked the idea, but what cemetery in its right mind would have permitted such frivolous nonsense? You're supposed to attend a funeral or visit a grave site to cry, not laugh. I figured any decent funeral home would have rejected my irreverent project faster than *Card Player* rejected one of my so-called vulgar articles.

But life often imitates art. Like the time I once made a satirical mention of a feminist deck, only to see one crop up for real years later. And now it seems my pipe dream poker funeral has become plausible.

What happened was that some friends and I took an annual tour of Hollywood Memorial Park Cemetery sponsored by the L.A. Art Deco Society, a non-profit group dedicated to preserving historic sites in the city. The cemetery is the last resting place of many early Hollywood notables, and it sounded like an interesting, if slightly morbid, safari.

Interesting it was. They have everyone interred here — from Douglas Fairbanks Sr. to Cecil B. DeMille to Tyrone Power, and the fanciful monuments range from Egyptian Revival to Moderne. One guy, who made his money in copper or something, built himself a mausoleum almost the size of the 131-unit condo complex I live in, surrounded by an enormous lake swarming with water fowl. (That's what I call living!)

But morbid the tour was not. It is always held just before Halloween, and the tip-off that it would be fun came when we were handed identifying plastic skeletons to attach to our clothing. Our host managed to get off plenty of oneliners. For example, Eleanor Holm, the tap dancer/actress, has her ashes in a bronze container shaped like a book. That, the guide explained, was so she could tell her friends to "Come down to the cemetery and check me out."

But what really got me excited was the sheer wackiness of

some of the memorials. For example, one guy had as his monument a huge stone rocket ship at least fifteen feet high. Was he connected with the space program in any way? Nope, he was just excited by rockets. Another gentleman had a strange diagram etched on his tombstone. It was the design of a machine he had invented ... a breast-enlargement machine!

There were some really cool sayings on the grave markers too. My absolute favorite was the one for Mel Blanc, who did all those cartoon voices. It read: "That's all, folks."

In other words, this is one great hang-loose cemetery where anything goes. Some of the stuff even made my poker funeral ravings look tame by comparison. So that's where I'm going to end up, for sure. Just think, I'll even be included in the tour, and I can give everyone a last good chuckle.

I've got to find something funnier than "Deal me out for a while," though. How about "Max Passes." Or ...